everyday

desserts

LOVE FOOD™

This edition published in 2010
LOVE FOOD is an imprint of Parragon Books Ltd

Parragon
Queen Street House
4 Queen Street
Bath BA1 1HE, UK

ISBN: 978-1-4054-8676-7

Printed in China

Designed by Terry Jeavons & Company

Notes for the Reader
This book uses both metric and imperial measurements. Follow the same units of measurement throughout; do not mix metric and imperial. All spoon measurements are level: teaspoons are assumed to be 5 ml, and tablespoons are assumed to be 15 ml. Unless otherwise stated, milk is assumed to be full fat, eggs and individual vegetables are medium, and pepper is freshly ground black pepper.

The times given are an approximate guide only. Preparation times differ according to the techniques used by different people and the cooking times may also vary from those given. Optional ingredients, variations or serving suggestions have not been included in the calculations.

Recipes using raw or very lightly cooked eggs should be avoided by infants, the elderly, pregnant women, convalescents and anyone suffering from an illness. Pregnant and breastfeeding women are advised to avoid eating peanuts and peanut products. Sufferers from nut allergies should be aware that some of the ready-made ingredients used in the recipes in this book may contain nuts. Always check the packaging before use.

everyday desserts

introduction

No matter how filling, and tasty, and satisfying your main dish is, there always seems to be just enough room left for dessert! If you are one of those people who cannot resist a sideways glance at the dessert trolley as it rolls past your table in your favourite restaurant, then this is the book for you.

A dessert is called upon to play many roles. A lovely, warming pudding, for example, is without doubt the ultimate comfort food. Think of the tantalizing aroma of a baked dessert as it comes out of the oven, irresistibly golden brown and crisp on top; or of a steamed pudding as you turn it out of the bowl, ready to be served dripping with sauce and absolutely delicious. Just the appetizing sight of the pudding alone is more than enough to cheer you on a cold day or when you are feeling out of sorts – and as for the taste …

Pies and tarts in all their guises are incredibly versatile – not only are they heavenly desserts, they also make perfect partners for morning coffee and afternoon tea, and are wonderful for late-night snacking.

Fruit-based desserts are ideal if you are serving a filling main dish but still want something sweet to round off the meal. They are also a great way to make the most of those seasonal fruits, such as summer berries, that are only available locally for a few short but very special weeks.

Chilled desserts, ice creams and refreshing sorbets are an elegant way to end a stylish dinner party at any time of year, and are an obvious choice for summer lunch parties, especially if you are eating alfresco. And of course a rich, creamy, delectable ice cream takes us back to comfort food – think of all those movies where the unhappy heroine and her friends tuck into giant tubs of their favourite flavour! When it's home-made, it's even better!

comfort puddings

A real 'comfort' pudding needs to be served hot from the oven or the steamer, have an aroma that is too tantalizing for words, look simply divine and taste absolutely out of this world. This winning combination will soon make your blues float away and even the most miserable weather will suddenly seem much brighter.

A comfort pudding means different things to different people. If chocolate is an essential ingredient, then try the Saucy Chocolate Pudding. It is light-as-a-feather, and bathed in an irresistibly rich sauce that you only discover when you spoon out the pudding. Or what about a melt-in-the-mouth Hot Chocolate Soufflé with Coffee Sabayon? It's baked in individual ramekins, and you might want more than one …

Warm, fruity comfort puddings always seem to be associated with harvest time, when the days become cooler and shorter and our thoughts turn to cosy evenings. Try the Apple and Blackberry Crumble if autumn is your favourite season.

Steamed puddings only need to be sniffed to cheer you up. Everything that is wonderful about a Syrup Sponge seems to get trapped in the steam that wafts up as you release it from its mould. And for complete but simple pleasure, the Creamy Rice Pudding, flavoured with vanilla, cannot be beaten.

saucy chocolate pudding

ingredients

SERVES 4–6

55 g/2 oz self-raising flour
25 g/1 oz cocoa powder
85 g/3 oz butter, softened, plus extra for greasing
1 tsp ground cinnamon
115 g/4 oz golden caster sugar
1 egg
2 tbsp dark brown sugar
55 g/2 oz pecan nuts, chopped
300 ml/10 fl oz hot black coffee
icing sugar, for dusting
whipped cream, to serve

method

1 Sift the flour, cocoa powder and cinnamon into a large bowl. Add the butter, 85 g/3 oz of the caster sugar and the egg and beat together until the mixture is well blended. Turn into a greased, shallow 1.2-litre/2¼-pint ovenproof dish and sprinkle with the dark brown sugar and the pecan nuts.

2 Pour the coffee into a large jug, stir in the remaining caster sugar until dissolved and carefully pour over the pudding.

3 Bake in a preheated oven, 160°C/325°F, for 50–60 minutes or until firm to the touch in the centre. Dust with a little icing sugar and serve with whipped cream.

bread & butter pudding

ingredients

SERVES 4–6

85 g/3 oz butter, softened
6 slices of thick white bread
55 g/2 oz mixed fruit (sultanas, currants and raisins)
25 g/1 oz candied peel
3 large eggs
300 ml/10 fl oz milk
150 ml/5 fl oz double cream
55 g/2 oz caster sugar
whole nutmeg, for grating
1 tbsp demerara sugar
cream, to serve

method

1 Use a little of the butter to grease a 20 x 25-cm/8 x 10-inch baking dish and use the remainder to butter the slices of bread. Cut the bread into quarters and arrange half overlapping in the dish.

2 Scatter half the dried fruit and candied peel over the bread, cover with the remaining bread slices and add the remaining dried fruit and candied peel.

3 In a jug, whisk the eggs well and mix in the milk, cream and sugar. Pour this over the pudding and stand for 15 minutes to allow the bread to soak up some of the egg mixture. Tuck in most of the fruit so that it doesn't burn. Grate the nutmeg over the top of the pudding, according to taste, and sprinkle over the demerara sugar.

4 Place the pudding on a baking sheet and bake at the top of a preheated oven, 180°C/350°F, for 30–40 minutes until just set and golden brown.

5 Serve warm with a little pouring cream.

panettone pudding

ingredients

SERVES 6

3 tbsp butter, softened, plus extra for greasing
250 g/9 oz panettone, cut into slices
225 ml/8 fl oz milk
225 ml/8 fl oz double cream
1 vanilla pod, split
3 eggs
115 g/4 oz golden caster sugar
2 tbsp apricot jam, warmed and strained

method

1 Grease an 850-ml/1 1/2-pint shallow ovenproof dish. Butter the slices of panettone and arrange in the dish. Place the milk, cream and vanilla pod in a saucepan over low heat and heat until the mixture reaches boiling point. Place the eggs and sugar in a bowl and beat together, then pour in the milk mixture and beat together.

2 Pour the custard through a sieve over the buttered panettone. Stand for 1 hour so that the panettone soaks up the custard. Preheat the oven to 160°C/325°F.

3 Bake the pudding in the preheated oven for 40 minutes, then drizzle the apricot jam over the top. If the top crusts of the dessert are not crisp and golden, heat under a preheated hot grill for 1 minute before serving.

german noodle pudding

ingredients

SERVES 4

4 tbsp butter, plus extra for greasing
175 g/6 oz ribbon egg noodles
115 g/4 oz cream cheese
225 g/8 oz cottage cheese
85 g/3 oz caster sugar
2 eggs, lightly beaten
125 ml/4 fl oz sour cream
1 tsp vanilla essence
pinch of ground cinnamon
1 tsp grated lemon rind
25 g/1 oz flaked almonds
25 g/1 oz dry white breadcrumbs
icing sugar, for dusting

method

1 Grease an ovenproof dish with a little butter. Bring a saucepan of water to the boil. Add the noodles, return to the boil and cook until almost tender. Drain and set aside.

2 Beat the cream cheese, cottage cheese and caster sugar together in a large bowl until the mixture is smooth. Beat in the eggs, a little at a time. Stir in the sour cream, vanilla essence, cinnamon and lemon rind and fold in the noodles. Transfer the mixture to the prepared dish and smooth the surface.

3 Melt the butter in a frying pan over low heat. Add the almonds and cook, stirring constantly, for 1–1½ minutes or until they are lightly coloured. Remove the pan from the heat and stir the breadcrumbs into the almonds.

4 Sprinkle the almond and breadcrumb mixture evenly over the pudding and bake in a preheated oven, 180°C/350°F, for 35–40 minutes or until just set. Dust the top with a little sifted icing sugar and serve.

upside-down pudding

ingredients

SERVES 6–8

225 g/8 oz unsalted butter
55 g/2 oz light brown sugar
14–16 hazelnuts
600 g/1 lb 5 oz canned apricot halves, drained
175 g/6 oz demerara sugar
3 eggs, beaten
175 g/6 oz self-raising flour
55 g/2 oz ground hazelnuts
2 tablespoons milk
cream or custard, to serve

method

1 Beat 55 g/2 oz of the butter with the light brown sugar and spread over the base of a greased and base-lined 25-cm/10-inch cake tin. Place a hazelnut in each apricot half and invert onto the base. The apricots should cover the whole surface.

2 Beat the demerara sugar together with the remaining butter until pale and fluffy, then gradually beat in the eggs. Fold in the flour, the ground hazelnuts and the milk and spread the mixture over the apricots.

3 Bake in the centre of a preheated oven, 180°C/350°F, for about 45 minutes or until the pudding is golden brown and well risen. Run a knife around the edge of the pudding and invert onto a warm serving plate. Serve warm with cream or custard.

chocolate cake with rosemary custard

ingredients

SERVES 8

- 150 g/5½ oz plain chocolate, broken into pieces
- 115 g/4 oz unsalted butter, plus extra for greasing
- 3 large eggs, separated, plus 1 extra egg white
- 115 g/4 oz golden caster sugar
- ¾ tsp cream of tartar
- 2 tbsp plain flour
- 1 tsp ground cinnamon
- 3 tbsp ground almonds
- icing sugar, for dusting
- fresh rosemary sprigs, to decorate

custard

- 2 fresh rosemary sprigs
- 1 vanilla pod, split
- 300 ml/10 fl oz single cream
- 150 ml/5 fl oz milk
- 5 large egg yolks
- 3 tbsp golden caster sugar

method

1 Melt the chocolate and butter in a heatproof bowl set over a pan of simmering water. Stir in the egg yolks and half the sugar. Place the egg whites and cream of tartar in a clean bowl and beat until soft peaks form. Gradually beat in the remaining sugar until stiff but not dry. Sift the flour and cinnamon into another bowl and stir in the almonds. Fold into the egg white mixture, then fold into the chocolate mixture.

2 Spoon the mixture into a greased and base-lined 22-cm/8½-inch round cake tin and stand in a roasting tin. Pour enough hot water into the roasting tin to come halfway up the sides of the cake tin. Bake in a preheated oven, 180°C/350°F, for about 1 hour or until firm to the touch. Remove from the roasting tin, cover, and stand for 10 minutes before turning out onto a wire rack to cool.

3 To make the custard, heat the rosemary, vanilla pod, cream and milk in a saucepan until almost boiling. Remove from the heat and infuse for 30 minutes. Beat the egg yolks and sugar together until thick and pale. Reheat the cream mixture, strain onto the egg mixture and whisk in. Set the bowl over a saucepan of simmering water and stir until thick. Dust the cake with icing sugar, decorate with rosemary and serve with the custard.

cherry & chocolate clafoutis

ingredients

SERVES 6–8

450 g/1 lb black cherries, pitted
butter, for greasing
2 tbsp golden granulated sugar
3 eggs
55 g/2 oz golden caster sugar
55 g/2 oz self-raising flour
2 tbsp cocoa powder
150 ml/5 fl oz cream
300 ml/10 fl oz milk
2 tbsp Kirsch (optional)
icing sugar, for dusting
fresh whole black cherries, to decorate
cream, to serve

method

1 Arrange the cherries in a greased 23-cm/9-inch ovenproof pie dish, sprinkle with the granulated sugar and set aside.

2 Place the eggs and caster sugar in a bowl and whisk together until light and frothy. Sift the flour and cocoa powder onto a plate and add, all at once, to the egg mixture. Beat in thoroughly, then whisk in the cream, followed by the milk and Kirsch, if using. Pour the batter over the cherries.

3 Bake in a preheated oven, 190°C/375°F, for 50–60 minutes or until slightly risen and set in the centre.

4 Dust with icing sugar and decorate with cherries. Serve warm with cream.

blackberry pudding

ingredients

SERVES 4

450 g/1 lb blackberries
75 g/2¾ oz caster sugar
6 tbsp butter, melted,
plus extra for greasing
1 egg
75 g/2¾ oz brown sugar
8 tbsp milk
125 g/4½ oz self-raising flour
sugar, for sprinkling

method

1 Gently mix the blackberries and caster sugar together in a large bowl, until combined. Transfer the mixture to a large ovenproof dish, lightly greased with butter.

2 Beat the egg and brown sugar in a separate mixing bowl. Stir in the melted butter and milk, then sift in the flour and fold together lightly with a figure-of-eight movement to form a smooth batter.

3 Carefully spread the batter over the blackberry and sugar mixture. Bake the pudding in a preheated oven, 180°C/350°F, for 25–30 minutes or until the topping is firm and golden. Sprinkle the pudding with sugar and serve hot.

peach cobbler

ingredients

SERVES 4–6

filling

6 peaches, peeled and sliced

4 tbsp caster sugar

½ tbsp lemon juice

1½ tsp cornflour

½ tsp almond or vanilla essence

vanilla or pecan ice cream, to serve

pie topping

185 g/6½ oz plain flour

115 g/4 oz caster sugar

1½ tsp baking powder

½ tsp salt

85 g/3 oz butter, diced

1 egg

6 tbsp milk

method

1 Place the peaches in a 23-cm/9-inch square ovenproof dish. Add the sugar, lemon juice, cornflour and almond essence and toss together. Bake in a preheated oven, 220°C/425°F, for 20 minutes.

2 Meanwhile, to make the topping, sift the flour, all but 2 tablespoons of the sugar, the baking powder and the salt into a bowl. Rub in the butter with the fingertips until the mixture resembles breadcrumbs. Mix the egg and 5 tablespoons of the milk in a jug, then mix into the dry ingredients with a fork until a soft, sticky dough forms. If the dough seems too dry, stir in the extra tablespoon of milk.

3 Reduce the oven temperature to 200°C/400°F. Remove the peaches from the oven and drop spoonfuls of the topping over the surface, without smoothing. Sprinkle with the remaining sugar, return to the oven and bake for a further 15 minutes or until the topping is golden brown and firm – the topping will spread as it cooks. Serve hot or at room temperature, with ice cream.

apple & blackberry crumble

ingredients

SERVES 6

450 g/1 lb cooking apples
450 g/1 lb blackberries
115 g/4 oz caster sugar
4 tbsp water
cream, yogurt or custard, to serve

crust

175 g/6 oz wholemeal flour
6 tbsp unsalted butter
85 g/3 oz light brown sugar
1 tsp mixed spice

method

1 Prepare the apples by cutting them into quarters, then peeling and coring them. Thinly slice them into an ovenproof dish. Add the blackberries and stir in the sugar, then pour in the water.

2 Make the crumble by placing the flour in a mixing bowl and rubbing in the butter until the mixture resembles breadcrumbs. Stir in the sugar and mixed spice. Spread the crumble evenly over the fruit and use a fork to press down lightly.

3 Place the dish on a baking sheet and bake in the centre of a preheated oven, 190°C/375°F, for 25–30 minutes or until the crumble is golden brown.

4 Serve warm with cream, yogurt or custard.

steamed chocolate pudding

ingredients

SERVES 4–6

115 g/4 oz butter, softened, plus extra for greasing
115 g/4 oz light brown sugar
2 eggs, beaten
85 g/3 oz self-raising flour
25 g/1 oz cocoa powder
1–2 tbsp milk (optional)
100 g/3½ oz plain chocolate chips

sauce

55 g/2 oz butter
55 g/2 oz light brown sugar
3 tbsp brandy
55 g/2 oz blanched whole hazelnuts
55 g/2 oz luxury mixed dried fruit

method

1 Grease a 1.2-litre/2-pint ovenproof bowl and line the base with a small circle of waxed paper. Beat the butter and sugar together until light and fluffy. Gradually beat in the eggs. Sift the flour and cocoa into the mixture and fold in. Add a little milk, if necessary, to make a dropping consistency. Stir in the chocolate chips.

2 Spoon the mixture into the prepared bowl. Cut out a circle of waxed paper and a circle of foil, both about 7.5 cm/3 inches larger than the top of the bowl. Place the paper on top of the foil and grease the upper surface. Make a fold in the centre of both, then use to cover the bowl, paper-side down and secure with string. Place the bowl on a trivet in a saucepan and pour in enough boiling water to come halfway up the sides of the bowl. Cover and simmer for 1½ hours, topping up with extra boiling water as necessary.

3 To make the sauce, place the butter and sugar in a small saucepan and heat gently until the sugar has dissolved and the mixture looks slightly caramelized. Add the brandy and let bubble for 1 minute. Stir in the hazelnuts and dried fruit. Carefully turn the pudding out onto a plate and spoon the sauce over. Serve immediately.

steamed syrup sponge pudding

ingredients

SERVES 6

115 g/4 oz butter, plus extra for greasing
2 tbsp golden syrup, plus extra to serve
115 g/4 oz caster sugar
2 eggs, lightly beaten
175 g/6 oz self-raising flour
2 tbsp milk
grated rind of 1 lemon

method

1 Butter a 1.2-litre/2-pint pudding basin and put the syrup into the bottom.

2 Beat together the butter and sugar until soft and creamy, then beat in the eggs, a little at a time. Fold in the flour and stir in the milk to make a soft dropping consistency. Add the lemon rind. Turn the mixture into the pudding basin. Cover the surface with a circle of wax paper or baking parchment and top with a pleated sheet of foil. Secure with some string or crimp the edges of the foil to ensure a tight fit around the bowl.

3 Place the pudding in a large saucepan half-filled with boiling water. Cover the pan and bring back to the boil over medium heat. Reduce the heat to a slow simmer and steam the pudding for $1^1/2$ hours until risen and firm. Keep checking the water level and top up with boiling water as necessary.

4 Remove the pan from the heat and lift out the pudding basin. Remove the cover and loosen the pudding from the sides of the basin using a knife. Turn out into a warmed dish and heat a little more syrup to serve with the pudding.

chocolate cranberry sponge

ingredients

SERVES 4

4 tbsp unsalted butter, plus extra for greasing
4 tbsp dark brown sugar, plus extra for sprinkling
85 g/3 oz cranberries, thawed if frozen
1 large cooking apple
2 eggs, lightly beaten
85 g/3 oz self-raising flour
3 tbsp cocoa powder

sauce

175 g/6 oz plain chocolate, broken into pieces
400 ml/14 fl oz evaporated milk
1 tsp vanilla essence
1/2 tsp almond essence

method

1 Grease a 1.2-litre/2-pint ovenproof bowl with a little butter, then sprinkle with brown sugar to coat the sides. Tip out any excess. Place the cranberries in a large bowl. Using a sharp knife, peel, core and dice the apple and mix with the cranberries, then place the fruit in the prepared bowl.

2 Place the butter, sugar and eggs in a large bowl. Sift in the flour and cocoa and beat until well mixed. Pour the mixture on top of the fruit. Cover the surface with a circle of waxed paper or baking parchment and top with a pleated sheet of foil, then tie with string. Place the bowl in a steamer set over a saucepan of simmering water and steam the pudding for 1 hour or until well risen, topping up with boiling water as necessary.

3 Meanwhile, make the sauce. Place the chocolate pieces and the milk in a heatproof bowl set over a saucepan of simmering water. Stir constantly until the chocolate has melted, then remove the bowl from the heat. Whisk in the vanilla and almond essences and beat until thick and smooth.

4 To serve, remove the pudding and discard the cover. Run a round-bladed knife round the side of the bowl, place a serving plate on top of the pudding and, holding them together, invert. Serve immediately with the sauce.

sticky toffee sponge

ingredients

SERVES 4

75 g/2¾ oz sultanas
150 g/5½ oz stoned dates, chopped
1 tsp bicarbonate of soda
2 tbsp butter, plus extra for greasing
200 g/7 oz brown sugar
2 eggs
200 g/7 oz self-raising flour, sifted
grated orange zest, to decorate
freshly whipped cream, to serve

sticky toffee sauce

2 tbsp butter
175 ml/6 fl oz double cream
200 g/7 oz brown sugar

method

1 To make the sponge, put the fruits and bicarbonate of soda into a heatproof bowl. Cover with boiling water and set aside to soak.

2 Put the butter in a separate bowl, add the sugar and mix well. Beat in the eggs, then fold in the flour. Drain the soaked fruits, add to the bowl and mix. Spoon the mixture evenly into a greased 20-cm/8-inch cake tin. Transfer to a preheated oven, 180°C/350°F and bake for 35–40 minutes. The sponge is cooked when a skewer inserted into the centre comes out clean. About 5 minutes before the end of the cooking time, make the sauce. Melt the butter in a saucepan over medium heat. Stir in the cream and sugar and bring to the boil, stirring constantly. Lower the heat and simmer for 5 minutes.

3 Turn out the sponge onto a serving plate and pour over the sauce. Decorate with grated orange zest and serve with whipped cream.

sticky coffee & walnut sponges

ingredients

SERVES 6

1 tbsp instant coffee powder
150 g/5½ oz self-raising flour
1 tsp ground cinnamon
55 g/2 oz butter, softened, plus extra for greasing
55 g/2 oz brown sugar, sifted
2 large eggs, beaten
55 g/2 oz finely chopped walnuts

butterscotch sauce

25 g/1 oz roughly chopped walnuts
55 g/2 oz butter
55 g/2 oz brown sugar
150 ml/5 fl oz double cream

method

1 Dissolve the coffee powder in 2 tablespoons of boiling water and set aside. Sift the flour and cinnamon into a bowl. Place the butter and sugar in a separate bowl and beat together until light and fluffy. Gradually beat in the eggs. Add a little flour if the mixture shows signs of curdling. Fold in half the flour and cinnamon mixture, then fold in the remaining flour and cinnamon, alternately with the coffee. Stir in the walnuts.

2 Divide the batter between 6 greased individual metal pudding bowls. Place a piece of buttered foil over each bowl and secure with an elastic band. Stand the bowls in a roasting tin and pour in enough boiling water to reach halfway up the sides of the bowls. Cover the roasting tin with a tent of foil, folding it under the rim.

3 Bake the sponges in a preheated oven, 190°C/375°F, for 30–40 minutes or until well risen and firm to the touch.

4 Meanwhile, make the sauce. Place all the ingredients in a saucepan over low heat and stir until melted and blended. Bring to a simmer, then remove from the heat. Turn the sponges out on to a serving plate, spoon over the hot sauce and serve.

individual chocolate puddings

ingredients

SERVES 4

100 g/3½ oz caster sugar
3 eggs
75 g/2¾ oz plain flour
50 g/1¾ oz cocoa powder
100 g/3½ oz unsalted butter, melted, plus extra for greasing
100 g/3½ oz plain chocolate, melted
coffee beans, to decorate

chocolate sauce

2 tbsp unsalted butter
100 g/3½ oz plain chocolate
5 tbsp water
1 tbsp caster sugar
1 tbsp coffee-flavoured liqueur, such as Kahlua

method

1 To make the puddings, put the sugar and eggs into a heatproof bowl and place over a saucepan of simmering water. Whisk for about 10 minutes until frothy. Remove the bowl from the heat and fold in the flour and cocoa. Fold in the butter, then the chocolate. Mix together thoroughly.

2 Grease 4 small heatproof bowls with butter. Spoon the mixture into the bowls and cover with waxed paper. Top with foil and secure with string. Place the puddings in a large saucepan filled with enough simmering water to reach halfway up the sides of the bowls. Steam for about 40 minutes or until cooked through.

3 About 2–3 minutes before the end of the cooking time, make the sauce. Put the butter, chocolate, water and sugar into a small pan and warm over low heat, stirring constantly, until melted together. Stir in the liqueur.

4 Remove the puddings from the heat, turn out into serving dishes and pour over the sauce. Decorate with coffee beans and serve.

individual chocolate fondant puddings

ingredients

SERVES 4

100 g/3½ oz butter, plus extra for greasing
100 g/3½ oz plain chocolate, broken into pieces
2 large eggs
1 tsp vanilla essence
100 g/3½ oz golden caster sugar, plus extra for coating
2 tbsp plain flour
icing sugar, for dusting
vanilla ice cream, to serve

method

1 Place the butter and chocolate in a heatproof bowl and set over a saucepan of gently simmering water until melted. Stir until smooth, then set aside to cool.

2 Place the eggs, vanilla essence, caster sugar and flour in a bowl and whisk together. Stir in the melted chocolate. Pour the mixture into 4 lightly greased 175-ml/6-fl oz ovenproof bowls or ramekins coated with caster sugar and place on a baking sheet. Bake in a preheated oven, 200°C/400°F, for 12–15 minutes or until the puddings are well risen and set on the outside but still melting inside.

3 Stand for 1 minute, then turn the puddings out on to 4 individual serving plates. Dust with icing sugar and serve immediately with vanilla ice cream.

grand marnier soufflé

ingredients

SERVES 4

55 g/2 oz caster sugar, plus a little extra for dusting
3 large eggs, separated, plus 1 large egg and 1 large egg white
4 tbsp plain flour
300 ml/10 fl oz milk
1/4 tsp vanilla essence
1/2 tbsp finely grated orange rind
2 1/2 tbsp Grand Marnier
1/4 tsp cream of tartar
butter, for greasing
icing sugar, to decorate

method

1 Using an electric mixer, beat the caster sugar, 1 whole egg and 1 egg yolk together until pale yellow and thoroughly blended. Stir in the flour, then slowly beat in the milk and vanilla essence.

2 Transfer to a heavy-based saucepan over medium-high heat and slowly bring to the boil, beating constantly, until a smooth, thick custard forms. Reduce the heat to low and simmer, still beating, for 2 minutes. Remove from the heat and beat in the remaining egg yolks, one by one, then cool slightly. Beat in the orange rind and Grand Marnier.

3 Meanwhile, wash and dry the mixer's beaters. Place the egg whites in a spotlessly clean bowl and beat on a low speed until frothy. Beat in the cream of tartar and continue whisking the egg whites until stiff peaks form.

4 Beat several tablespoons of the egg whites into the custard to loosen, add the custard mixture to the egg whites and use a metal spoon to fold the mixtures together, lightly but quickly, using a figure-of-eight motion.

5 Spoon the mixture into a 1.75-litre/3-pint soufflé dish greased with butter and sprinkled with a little caster sugar. Transfer the dish to a preheated baking sheet and bake in a preheated oven, 180°C/350°F, for 45 minutes or until well risen and golden. Dust with icing sugar and serve at once.

cappuccino soufflé puddings

ingredients

SERVES 6

6 tbsp whipping cream
2 tsp instant espresso coffee granules
2 tbsp Kahlua
butter, for greasing
2 tbsp golden caster sugar, plus extra for coating
3 large eggs, separated, plus 1 extra egg white
150 g/5½ oz plain chocolate, melted and cooled
cocoa powder, for dusting
vanilla ice cream, to serve

method

1 Place the cream in a small, heavy-based saucepan and heat gently. Stir in the coffee until it has dissolved, then stir in the Kahlua. Divide the coffee mixture between 6 lightly greased 175-ml/6-fl oz ramekins coated with caster sugar.

2 Place the egg whites in a clean, greasefree bowl and whisk until soft peaks form, then gradually whisk in the sugar until stiff but not dry. Stir the egg yolks and melted chocolate together in a separate bowl, then stir in a little of the whisked egg whites. Gradually fold in the remaining egg whites.

3 Divide the mixture between the ramekins. Place the ramekins on a baking sheet and bake in a preheated oven, 190°C/375°F, for 15 minutes or until just set. Dust with sifted cocoa powder and serve immediately with vanilla ice cream.

hot chocolate soufflé with coffee sabayon

ingredients

SERVES 4–6

3 tbsp cornflour
250 ml/9 fl oz milk
115 g/4 oz plain chocolate, broken into pieces
4 eggs, separated
55 g/2 oz golden caster sugar, plus extra for coating
butter, for greasing
icing sugar, for dusting

sabayon

2 eggs
3 egg yolks
85 g/3 oz golden caster sugar
4 tsp instant coffee granules
2 tbsp brandy

method

1 To make the soufflé, place the cornflour in a bowl. Add a little milk and stir until smooth. Pour the remaining milk into a heavy-based saucepan and add the chocolate. Heat gently until the chocolate has melted, then stir. Pour the chocolate milk onto the cornflour paste, stirring. Return to the pan and bring to the boil, stirring. Simmer for 1 minute. Remove from the heat and stir in the egg yolks, one at a time. Cover and cool slightly.

2 Place the egg whites in a large, spotlessly clean bowl and whisk until soft peaks form. Gradually whisk in the caster sugar until stiff but not dry. Stir a little of the mixture into the chocolate mixture, then carefully fold in the the remainder. Pour into a greased 1-litre/ 1¾-pint soufflé dish coated with caster sugar, then bake in a preheated oven, 190°C/375°F, for 40 minutes or until it is well risen and wobbles slightly when pushed.

3 Just before the soufflé is ready, make the coffee sabayon. Place all the ingredients in a heavy-based saucepan over very low heat and cook, whisking constantly, until the mixture is thick and light. Dust a little icing sugar over the soufflé and serve immediately, with the sabayon.

queen of puddings

ingredients

SERVES 8

600 ml/1 pint milk
2 tbsp butter, plus extra for greasing
225 g/8 oz caster sugar
finely grated rind of 1 orange
4 eggs, separated
85 g/3 oz fresh white breadcrumbs
pinch of salt
6 tbsp orange marmalade

method

1 To make the custard, gently heat the milk in a saucepan with the butter, 75 g/2½ oz of the sugar and the grated orange rind until just warm.

2 Whisk the egg yolks in a bowl. Gradually pour the warm milk over the eggs, stirring constantly. Stir the breadcrumbs into the custard, then transfer the mixture to a greased ovenproof dish and stand for about 15 minutes.

3 Bake in a preheated oven, 180°C/350°F, for 20–25 minutes or until the custard has just set. Remove the dish from the oven, but do not turn off the oven.

4 To make the meringue, whisk the egg whites with the salt in a clean, greasefree bowl until soft peaks form. Whisk in the remaining sugar, a little at a time.

5 When cool, gently spread the orange marmalade over the cooked custard. Use a palette knife to spread over the meringue in little peaks, or pipe the meringue on top.

6 Return the pudding to the oven and bake for a further 20 minutes until the meringue is crisp and golden. Serve warm.

creamy rice pudding

ingredients

SERVES 4

85 g/3 oz sultanas
5 tbsp caster sugar
90 g/3¼ oz pudding rice
1.2 litres/2 pints milk
1 tsp vanilla essence
1 tbsp butter, for greasing
finely grated zest of 1 large lemon
pinch of nutmeg
chopped pistachios, to decorate

method

1 Put the sultanas, sugar and rice into a mixing bowl, then stir in the milk and vanilla essence. Transfer to a greased 850-ml/1½-pint ovenproof dish, sprinkle over the grated lemon zest and the nutmeg, then bake in a preheated oven, 160°C/325°F, for 2½ hours.

2 Remove from the oven and transfer to individual serving bowls. Decorate with chopped pistachios and serve.

pies & tarts

The person who invented pastry deserves a word of thanks from us all, because without it we would never experience the pleasure of an incredible range of delicious fillings encased in a crisp, delicious crust.

One of the tastiest ways to use pastry is in a fruit pie. There are lots of ideas to choose from here, from the wonderful Traditional Apple Pie – be generous with the spices, both for aroma and taste – to the glorious Fig, Ricotta and Honey Tart with its sunshine flavour of the Mediterranean. To ring the changes, try the Paper-thin Fruit Pies – the fruit nestles in a crisp 'nest' of filo pastry – or the 'upside-down' Peach and Preserved Ginger Tarte Tatin.

If you want a pie that is completely and utterly indulgent, try Banoffee Pie. It sits on a crisp, nutty, biscuit base and although you need to set aside a couple of hours for the condensed milk to simmer, it is quick to make, but looks impressively complicated. Crème Brûlée Tarts are double heaven – a really special dessert in its own right, the custard is even better served in a shell.

If you are in a hurry but still want to bake a pie, choose a recipe where you can use ready-made pastry – you'll still have all the pleasure of rolling it out!

banoffee pie

ingredients

SERVES 4

filling

3 x 400 g/14 oz cans sweetened condensed milk
4 ripe bananas
juice of 1/2 lemon
1 tsp vanilla essence
75 g/2 3/4 oz plain chocolate, grated
475 ml/16 fl oz double cream, whipped

biscuit crust

85 g/3 oz butter, melted, plus extra for greasing
150 g/5 1/2 oz digestive biscuits, crushed into crumbs
25 g/1 oz almonds, toasted and ground
25 g/1 oz hazelnuts, toasted and ground

method

1 Place the unopened cans of milk in a large saucepan and add enough water to cover them. Bring to the boil, then reduce the heat and simmer for 2 hours, topping up the water level to keep the cans covered. Carefully lift out the hot cans from the pan and cool.

2 To make the crust, place the butter in a bowl and add the crushed digestive biscuits and ground nuts. Mix together well, then press the mixture evenly into the base and sides of a greased 23-cm/9-inch tart tin. Bake in a preheated oven, 180°C/350°F, for 10–12 minutes, then remove from the oven and cool.

3 Peel and slice the bananas and place in a bowl. Squeeze over the juice from the lemon, add the vanilla essence and mix together. Spread the banana mixture over the biscuit crust in the pan, then spoon over the contents of the cooled cans of condensed milk.

4 Sprinkle over 50 g/1 3/4 oz of the chocolate, then top with a layer of whipped cream. Sprinkle over the remaining grated chocolate and serve the pie at room temperature.

pecan pie

ingredients

SERVES 8

pastry

250 g/9 oz plain flour
pinch of salt
115 g/4 oz butter, cut into small pieces
1 tbsp lard or vegetable shortening, cut into small pieces
55 g/2 oz golden caster sugar
6 tbsp cold milk

filling

3 eggs
250 g/9 oz muscovado sugar
1 tsp vanilla essence
pinch of salt
85 g/3 oz butter, melted
3 tbsp golden syrup
3 tbsp molasses
350 g/12 oz pecan nuts, roughly chopped

pecan halves, to decorate
whipped cream or vanilla ice cream, to serve

method

1 To make the pastry, sift the flour and salt into a mixing bowl and rub in the butter and lard with the fingertips until the mixture resembles fine breadcrumbs. Work in the caster sugar and add the milk. Work the mixture into a soft dough. Wrap the pastry and chill in the refrigerator for 30 minutes.

2 Roll out the pastry and use it to line a 23–25-cm/9–10-inch tart tin. Trim off the excess by running the rolling pin over the top of the tart tin. Line with baking parchment and fill with baking beans. Bake in a preheated oven, 200°C/400°F, for 20 minutes. Take out of the oven and remove the paper and beans. Reduce the oven temperature to 180°C/350°F. Place a baking sheet in the oven.

3 To make the filling, place the eggs in a bowl and beat lightly. Beat in the muscovado sugar, vanilla essence and salt. Stir in the butter, syrup, molasses and chopped nuts. Pour into the pastry case and decorate with the pecan halves.

4 Place on the heated baking sheet and bake in the oven for 35-40 minutes until the filling is set. Serve warm or at room temperature with whipped cream or vanilla ice cream.

mississippi mud pie

ingredients

SERVES 8

pastry

250 g/9 oz plain flour, plus extra for dusting
2 tbsp cocoa powder
140 g/5 oz butter
2 tbsp caster sugar
1–2 tbsp cold water

filling

175 g/6 oz butter
250 g/9 oz brown sugar
4 eggs, lightly beaten
4 tbsp cocoa powder, sifted
150 g/5½ oz plain chocolate
300 ml/10 fl oz single cream
1 tsp chocolate extract

to decorate

425 ml/15 fl oz double cream, whipped
chocolate flakes and curls

method

1 To make the pastry, sift the flour and cocoa into a mixing bowl. Rub in the butter with the fingertips until the mixture resembles fine breadcrumbs. Stir in the sugar and enough cold water to mix to a soft dough. Wrap and chill in the refrigerator for 15 minutes.

2 Roll out the pastry on a lightly floured work surface and use to line a 23-cm/9-inch loose-based tart tin or ceramic pie dish. Line with baking parchment and fill with baking beans. Bake in a preheated oven, 190°C/375°F, for 15 minutes. Remove from the oven and take out the paper and beans. Bake the pastry case for a further 10 minutes.

3 To make the filling, beat the butter and sugar together in a bowl and gradually beat in the eggs with the cocoa. Melt the chocolate and beat it into the mixture with the single cream and the chocolate extract.

4 Reduce the oven temperature to 160°C/325°F. Pour the mixture into the pastry case and bake for 45 minutes or until the filling has set gently. Cool completely, then transfer to a serving plate.

5 Cover the mud pie with the whipped cream, decorate with chocolate flakes and curls and chill until ready to serve.

chocolate chiffon pie

ingredients

SERVES 8

nut base

225 g/8 oz whole Brazil nuts
4 tbsp granulated sugar
4 tsp melted butter

filling

225 ml/8 fl oz milk
2 tsp powdered gelatine
115 g/4 oz caster sugar
2 eggs, separated
225 g/8 oz plain chocolate, roughly chopped
1 tsp vanilla essence
150 ml/5 fl oz double cream
2 tbsp chopped Brazil nuts, to decorate

method

1 To make the base, process the whole Brazil nuts in a food processor until finely ground. Add the sugar and melted butter and process briefly to combine. Tip the mixture into a 23-cm/9-inch round tart tin and press it onto the base and side with a spoon. Bake in a preheated oven, 200°C/400°F, for 8–10 minutes or until light golden brown, then cool.

2 Pour the milk into a bowl and sprinkle over the gelatine. Let it soften for 2 minutes, then set over a saucepan of gently simmering water. Stir in half of the caster sugar, both the egg yolks and all the chocolate. Stir constantly over low heat for 4–5 minutes until the gelatine has dissolved and the chocolate has melted. Remove from the heat and beat until the mixture is smooth. Stir in the vanilla essence, wrap and chill in the refrigerator for 45–60 minutes until starting to set.

3 Whip the cream until it is stiff, then fold all but 3 tablespoons into the chocolate mixture. Whisk the egg whites in a separate, clean, greasefree bowl until soft peaks form. Add 2 teaspoons of the remaining sugar and whisk until stiff peaks form. Fold in the remaining sugar, then fold the egg whites into the chocolate mixture. Pour the filling into the nut case and chill in the refrigerator for 3 hours. Decorate with the remaining whipped cream and the chopped nuts before serving.

custard pie

ingredients

SERVES 8

pastry

200 g/7 oz plain flour
2 tbsp caster sugar
115 g/4 oz butter,
cut into small pieces
1 tbsp water

filling

3 eggs
85 g/3 oz caster sugar
150 ml/5 fl oz single cream
150 ml/5 fl oz milk
freshly grated nutmeg

whipped cream (optional),
to serve

method

1 To make the pastry, place the flour and sugar in a mixing bowl. Rub in the butter with the fingertips until the mixture resembles fine breadcrumbs. Add the water and mix together until a soft dough has formed. Wrap the pastry and chill in the refrigerator for 30 minutes, then roll out to a circle slightly larger than a 24-cm/9½-inch loose-based tart tin.

2 Line the tin with the pastry, trimming off the edge. Prick all over the base with a fork and chill in the refrigerator for about 30 minutes.

3 Line the pastry case with baking parchment and fill with baking beans. Bake in a preheated oven, 190°C/375°F, for 15 minutes. Remove the paper and beans and bake the pastry case for a further 15 minutes.

4 To make the filling, whisk the eggs, sugar, cream, milk and nutmeg together. Pour the filling into the prepared pastry case.

5 Return the pie to the oven and cook for a further 25–30 minutes or until the filling is just set. Serve with whipped cream, if you like.

forest fruit pie

ingredients

SERVES 4

filling

225 g/8 oz blueberries
225 g/8 oz raspberries
225 g/8 oz blackberries
100 g/3½ oz caster sugar

pastry

225 g/8 oz plain flour, plus extra for dusting
25 g/1 oz ground hazelnuts
100 g/3½ oz butter, cut into small pieces, plus extra for greasing
finely grated rind of 1 lemon
1 egg yolk, beaten
4 tbsp milk

2 tbsp icing sugar, to decorate
whipped cream, to serve

method

1 Place the fruit in a heavy-based saucepan with 3 tablespoons of the caster sugar and simmer gently, stirring frequently, for 5 minutes. Remove the pan from the heat.

2 Sift the flour into a bowl, then add the hazelnuts. Rub in the butter with the fingertips until the mixture resembles breadcrumbs, then sift in the remaining sugar. Add the lemon rind, egg yolk and 3 tablespoons of the milk and mix. Turn out on to a lightly floured work surface and knead briefly. Wrap and chill in the refrigerator for 30 minutes.

3 Grease a 20-cm/8-inch pie dish with butter. Roll out two-thirds the pastry to a thickness of 5 mm/¼ inch and use it to line the base and side of the dish. Spoon the fruit into the pastry case. Brush the rim with water, then roll out the remaining pastry to cover the pie. Trim and crimp round the edge, then make 2 small slits in the top and decorate with 2 leaf shapes cut out from the pastry trimmings. Brush all over with the remaining milk. Bake in a preheated oven, 190°C/375°F, for 40 minutes.

4 Remove from the oven, sprinkle with the icing sugar and serve with whipped cream.

traditional apple pie

ingredients

SERVES 6

pastry

350 g/12 oz plain flour
pinch of salt
85 g/3 oz butter or margarine, cut into small pieces
85 g/3 oz lard or vegetable shortening, cut into small pieces
about 6 tbsp cold water
beaten egg or milk, for glazing

filling

750 g–1 kg /1 lb 10 oz–2 lb 4 oz cooking apples, peeled, cored and sliced
115 g/4 oz brown or caster sugar, plus extra for sprinkling
$^{1}/_{2}$–1 tsp ground cinnamon, allspice or ground ginger
1–2 tbsp water (optional)

whipped double cream, to serve

method

1 To make the pastry, sift the flour and salt into a large bowl. Add the butter and fat and rub in with the fingertips until the mixture resembles fine breadcrumbs. Add the water and gather the mixture together into a dough. Wrap the pastry and chill in the refrigerator for 30 minutes.

2 Roll out almost two-thirds of the pastry thinly and use to line a deep 23-cm/9-inch pie plate or pie tin.

3 Mix the apples with the sugar and spice and pack into the pastry case; the filling can come up above the rim. Add the water if needed, particularly if the apples are a dry variety.

4 Roll out the remaining pastry to form a lid. Dampen the edges of the pie rim with water and position the lid, pressing the edges firmly together. Trim and crimp the edges.

5 Use the trimmings to cut out leaves or other shapes to decorate the top of the pie, dampen and attach. Glaze the top of the pie with beaten egg or milk, make 1–2 slits in the top and place the pie on a baking sheet.

6 Bake in a preheated oven, 220°C/425°F, for 20 minutes, then reduce the temperature to 180°C/350°F and bake for a further 30 minutes or until the pastry is a light golden brown. Serve hot or cold, sprinkled with sugar, with whipped cream.

apple lattice pie

ingredients

SERVES 4

pastry

280 g/10 oz plain flour, plus extra for dusting
pinch of salt
55 g/2 oz caster sugar
250 g/9 oz butter, cut into small pieces
1 egg
1 egg yolk
1 tbsp water

filling

3 tbsp blackcurrant or plum jam
55 g/2 oz chopped toasted mixed nuts
950 g/2 lb 2 oz cooking apples
1 tbsp lemon juice
1 tsp mixed spice
55 g/2 oz sultanas
50 g/1$^{3}/_{4}$ oz grapes, halved and seeded
75 g/2$^{3}/_{4}$ oz brown sugar

icing sugar, for dusting
custard, to serve

method

1 To make the pastry, sift the flour and salt into a bowl. Make a well in the centre and add the sugar, butter, egg, egg yolk and water. Mix together to form a smooth dough, adding more water if necessary. Wrap the pastry and chill in the refrigerator for 1 hour.

2 Shape about three-quarters of the pastry into a ball and roll out on a lightly floured work surface into a circle large enough to line a shallow 25-cm/10-inch tart tin. Fit it into the tin and trim the edge. Roll out the remaining pastry and cut into long strips about 1 cm/ $^{1}/_{2}$ inch wide.

3 To make the filling, spread the jam evenly over the base of the pastry case, then sprinkle over the toasted nuts. Peel and core the apples, then cut them into thin slices. Place them in a bowl with the lemon juice, mixed spice, sultanas, grapes and brown sugar. Mix together gently. Spoon the mixture into the pastry case, spreading it out evenly.

4 Arrange the pastry strips in a lattice over the top of the pie. Moisten with a little water, seal and trim the edges. Bake in a preheated oven, 200°C/400°F, for 50 minutes or until golden. Dust with icing sugar. Serve at once with custard.

pear pie

ingredients

SERVES 6

pastry

280 g/10 oz plain flour
pinch of salt
125 g/4 oz caster sugar
115 g/4 oz butter, cut into small pieces
1 egg
1 egg yolk
few drops vanilla essence
2–3 tsp water

filling

4 tbsp apricot jam
55 g/2 oz amaretti or ratafia biscuits, crumbled
850 g–1 kg/1 lb 14 oz–2 lb 4 oz pears, peeled and cored
1 tsp ground cinnamon
85 g/3 oz raisins
85 g/3 oz brown or raw sugar

sifted icing sugar, for sprinkling

method

1 To make the pastry, sift the flour and salt on to a work surface, make a well in the centre and add the sugar, butter, egg, egg yolk, vanilla essence and most of the water. Using your fingers, gradually work the flour into the other ingredients to form a smooth dough, adding more water if necessary. Wrap the pastry and chill in the refrigerator for at least 1 hour.

2 Roll out three-quarters of the pastry and use to line a shallow 25-cm/10-inch cake tin or deep tart tin. To make the filling, spread the jam over the base and sprinkle with the crushed biscuits.

3 Slice the pears very thinly. Arrange over the biscuits in the pastry case. Sprinkle with cinnamon, then with raisins and, finally, with brown sugar.

4 Roll out a thin sausage shape using a third of the remaining pastry and place around the edge of the pie. Roll the remainder into thin sausages and arrange in a lattice over the pie, 4 or 5 strips in each direction, attaching them to the strip around the edge.

5 Cook in a preheated oven, 200°C/400°F, for 50 minutes until golden brown and cooked through. Cool, then serve warm or chilled, sprinkled with sifted icing sugar.

lemon meringue pie

ingredients

SERVES 4

pastry

185 g/6½ oz plain flour, plus extra for dusting
85 g/3 oz butter, cut into small pieces, plus extra for greasing
55 g/2 oz icing sugar, sifted
finely grated rind of ½ lemon
½ egg yolk, beaten
1½ tbsp milk

filling

3 tbsp cornflour
300 ml/10 fl oz water
juice and grated rind of 2 lemons
185 g/6 oz caster sugar
2 eggs, separated

method

1 To make the pastry, sift the flour into a bowl. Rub in the butter with the fingertips until the mixture resembles fine breadcrumbs. Mix in the remaining ingredients. Knead briefly on a lightly floured work surface. Chill in the refrigerator for 30 minutes.

2 Grease a 20-cm/8-inch pie dish with butter. Roll out the pastry to a thickness of 5 mm/¼ inch; use it to line the base and sides of the dish. Prick all over with a fork, line with baking parchment and fill with baking beans. Bake for in a preheated oven, 180°C/350°F, for 15 minutes. Remove from the oven and take out the paper and beans. Reduce the temperature to 150°C/300°F.

3 To make the filling, mix the cornflour with a little of the water. Place the remaining water in a saucepan. Stir in the lemon juice and rind and cornflour paste. Bring to the boil, stirring. Cook for 2 minutes, then cool a little. Stir in 5 tablespoons of the sugar and the egg yolks and pour into the pastry case.

4 Whisk the egg whites in a clean, greasefree bowl until stiff. Whisk in the remaining sugar and spread over the pie. Bake for another 40 minutes. Remove from the oven, cool and serve.

paper-thin fruit pies

ingredients

MAKES 4

1 eating apple
1 ripe pear
2 tbsp lemon juice
4 tbsp melted butter
4 sheets filo pastry, thawed if frozen
2 tbsp apricot jam
1 tbsp unsweetened orange juice
1 tbsp finely chopped pistachios
2 tsp icing sugar, for dusting
custard, to serve

method

1 Core and thinly slice the apple and pear and immediately toss them in the lemon juice to prevent them from turning brown. Melt the butter in a pan over low heat.

2 Cut each sheet of pastry into 4 and cover with a clean, damp tea towel. Brush a 4-cup muffin pan (cup size 10 cm/4 inches in diameter) with a little of the butter.

3 Brush 4 small sheets of pastry with melted butter. Press a sheet of pastry into the base of 1 cup. Arrange the other sheets of pastry on top at slightly different angles. Repeat with the other sheets of pastry to make another 3 pies.

4 Arrange alternate slices of apple and pear in the centre of each pastry case and lightly crimp the edges of the pastry.

5 Stir the jam and orange juice together until smooth and brush over the fruit. Bake in a preheated oven, 200°C/400°F, for 12–15 minutes. Sprinkle with the pistachios, dust lightly with icing sugar and serve hot straight from the oven with custard.

maple pecan pies

ingredients

MAKES 12

pastry

150 g/5½ oz plain flour, plus extra for dusting
85 g/3 oz butter, cut into small pieces
55 g/2 oz golden caster sugar
2 egg yolks

filling

2 tbsp maple syrup
150 ml/5 fl oz double cream
115 g/4 oz golden caster sugar
pinch of cream of tartar
6 tbsp water
185 g/6 oz pecans, chopped
12 pecan halves, to decorate

method

1 To make the pastry, sift the flour into a mixing bowl and rub in the butter with the fingertips until the mixture resembles breadcrumbs. Add the sugar and egg yolks and mix to form a soft dough. Wrap the pastry and chill in the refrigerator for 30 minutes.

2 On a lightly floured work surface, roll out the pastry thinly, cut out 12 circles and use to line 12 tartlet pans. Prick the bases with a fork. Line with baking parchment and fill with baking beans. Bake in a preheated oven, 200°C/400°F, for 10–15 minutes or until light golden. Remove from the oven and take out the paper and beans. Bake the pastry cases for 2–3 minutes more. Cool on a wire rack.

3 Mix half the maple syrup and half the cream in a bowl. Place the sugar, cream of tartar and water in a saucepan and heat gently until the sugar dissolves. Bring to the boil and boil until light golden. Remove from the heat and stir in the maple syrup and cream mixture.

4 Return the pan to the heat and cook until a little of the mixture dropped into a bowl of cold water forms a soft ball. Stir in the remaining cream and leave until cool. Brush the remaining maple syrup over the edges of the pies. Place the chopped pecans in the pastry cases and spoon in the toffee. Top each pie with a pecan half. Cool completely before serving.

fig, ricotta & honey tart

ingredients

SERVES 6

pastry

150 g/5½ oz plain flour
pinch of salt
75 g/2¾ oz cold butter, cut into pieces
25 g/1 oz ground almonds
cold water

filling

6 figs
100 g/3½ oz caster sugar
600 ml/1 pint water
4 egg yolks
½ tsp vanilla essence
500 g/1 lb 2 oz ricotta cheese, drained of any liquid
2 tbsp flower honey, plus 1 tsp for drizzling

method

1 Lightly grease a 22-cm/9-inch loose-based fluted tart tin. Sift the flour and salt into a food processor, add the butter and process until the mixture resembles fine breadcrumbs. Tip the mixture into a bowl, stir in the almonds and add just enough cold water to bring the pastry together. Turn out onto a floured work surface and roll out the pastry 8 cm/3¼ inches larger than the tin. Carefully lift the pastry into the tin and press to fit. Roll the rolling pin over the tin to neaten the edges and trim the excess pastry. Fit a piece of baking parchment into the pastry case, fill with baking beans and chill for 30 minutes.

2 Remove the pastry case from the refrigerator and bake for 15 minutes in a preheated oven, 190°C/375°F, then remove the beans and paper. Return to the oven for a further 5 minutes.

3 Put the figs, half the caster sugar and the water in a saucepan and bring to the boil. Poach gently for 10 minutes, drain and cool. Stir the egg yolks and vanilla essence into the ricotta, add the remaining sugar and the honey and mix well. Spoon into the pastry case and bake for 30 minutes. Remove from the oven and, when you are ready to serve, cut the figs in half lengthways and arrange on the tart, cut-side up. Drizzle with the extra honey and serve at once.

honey and lemon tart

ingredients

SERVES 8–12

pastry

225 g/8 oz plus 3 tbsp plain flour
pinch of salt
$1^1/_2$ tsp caster sugar
150 g/$5^1/_2$ oz butter
3-4 tbsp cold water

filling

375 g/13 oz cottage cheese, cream cheese or ricotta
6 tbsp Greek honey
3 eggs, beaten
$^1/_2$ tsp cinnamon
grated rind and juice of 1 lemon

lemon slices, to decorate

method

1 To make the pastry, put the flour, salt, sugar and butter, cut into cubes, in a food processor. Mix in short bursts, until the mixture resembles fine breadcrumbs. Sprinkle over the water and mix until the mixture forms a smooth dough. Alternatively, make the pastry in a bowl and rub in with your hands. Wrap the pastry and chill in the refrigerator for 30 minutes.

2 Meanwhile, make the filling. (If using cottage cheese, push the cheese through a sieve into a bowl.) Add the honey to the cheese and beat until smooth. Add the eggs, cinnamon and the lemon rind and juice and mix well.

3 On a lightly floured work surface, roll out the pastry and use to line a 22-cm/9-inch tart tin. Place on a baking sheet and line with waxed paper. Fill with baking beans and bake in a preheated oven, 200°C/400°F, for 15 minutes. Remove the waxed paper and beans and bake for a further 5 minutes or until the base is firm but not brown.

4 Reduce the oven temperature to 180°C/350°F. Pour the filling into the pastry case and bake in the oven for about 30 minutes until set. Serve cold.

plum & almond tart

ingredients

SERVES 8

butter, for greasing
plain flour, for dusting
400 g/14 oz ready-made sweet pastry

filling

1 egg
1 egg yolk
140 g/5 oz golden caster sugar
55 g/2 oz butter, melted
100 g/3½ oz ground almonds
1 tbsp brandy
900 g/2 lb plums, halved and pitted

whipped cream, to serve (optional)

method

1 Grease a 23-cm/9-inch tart tin. On a lightly floured work surface, roll out the pastry and use it to line the tart tin. Line with baking parchment and fill with baking beans, then bake in a preheated oven, 200°C/400°F, for 15 minutes. Remove the paper and beans and return to the oven for a further 5 minutes. Place a baking sheet in the oven.

2 To make the filling, place the egg, egg yolk, 100g/3½ oz of the caster sugar, melted butter, ground almonds and brandy in a bowl and mix together to form a paste. Spread the paste in the pastry case.

3 Arrange the plum halves, cut-side up, on top of the almond paste, fitting them together tightly. Sprinkle with the remaining caster sugar. Place the tart tin on the preheated baking sheet and bake for 35–40 minutes or until the filling is set and the pastry case is brown. Serve warm with whipped cream, if you like.

bakewell tart

ingredients

SERVES 4

pastry

150 g/5½ oz plain flour, plus extra for dusting

50 g/1¾ oz butter, cut into small pieces, plus extra for greasing

25 g/1 oz icing sugar, sifted

finely grated rind of ½ lemon

½ egg yolk, beaten

1½ tbsp milk

4 tbsp strawberry jam

filling

100 g/3½ oz butter

100 g/3½ oz brown sugar

2 eggs, beaten

1 tsp almond essence

115 g/4 oz rice flour

3 tbsp ground almonds

3 tbsp flaked almonds, toasted

icing sugar, to decorate

method

1 To make the pastry, sift the flour into a bowl. Rub in the butter with the fingertips until the mixture resembles fine breadcrumbs. Mix in the icing sugar, lemon rind, egg yolk and milk. Knead briefly on a lightly floured work surface. Wrap the pastry and chill in the refrigerator for 30 minutes.

2 Grease a 20-cm/8-inch ovenproof tart tin. Roll out the pastry to a thickness of 5 mm/ ¼ inch and use it to line the base and side of the tin. Prick all over the base with a fork, then spread with the jam.

3 To make the filling, cream the butter and sugar together until fluffy. Gradually beat in the eggs, followed by the almond essence, rice flour and ground almonds. Spread the mixture evenly over the jam-covered pastry, then sprinkle over the flaked almonds. Bake in a preheated oven, 190°C/375°F, for 40 minutes until golden. Remove from the oven, dust with icing sugar and serve warm.

almond tart

ingredients

SERVES 8–12

pastry

280 g/10 oz plain flour
150 g/5½ oz caster sugar
1 tsp finely grated lemon rind
pinch of salt
150 g/5½ oz unsalted butter, chilled and cut into small dice
1 medium egg, beaten lightly
1 tbsp chilled water

filling

175 g/6 oz unsalted butter, at room temperature
175 g/6 oz caster sugar
3 large eggs
175 g/6 oz finely ground almonds
2 tsp plain flour
1 tbsp finely grated orange rind
½ tsp almond essence

icing sugar, to decorate
crème fraîche (optional), to serve

method

1 First, make the pastry. Put the flour, sugar, lemon rind and salt in a bowl. Rub or cut in the butter until the mixture resembles fine breadcrumbs. Combine the egg and water, then slowly pour into the flour, stirring with a fork until a coarse dough forms. Shape into a ball and chill for at least 1 hour.

2 Roll out the pastry on a lightly floured work surface until 3 mm/⅛ inch thick. Use to line a greased 25-cm/10-inch tart tin with a removable base. Return the tart tin to the refrigerator for at least 15 minutes.

3 Cover the pastry case with foil and fill with baking beans. Bake in a preheated oven, 220°C/425°F, for 12 minutes. Remove the beans and foil and return the pastry case to the oven for 4 minutes to dry the base. Remove from the oven and reduce the oven temperature to 200°C/400°F.

4 To make the filling, beat the butter and sugar until creamy. Beat in the eggs, 1 at a time. Add the almonds, flour, orange rind and almond essence and beat until blended. Spoon into the pastry case and smooth the surface. Bake for 30–35 minutes until the top is golden and the tip of a knife inserted in the centre comes out clean. Cool completely on a wire rack, then dust with icing sugar. Serve with a spoonful of crème fraîche, if wished.

coconut tart

ingredients

SERVES 8

plain flour, for dusting
400 g/14 oz ready-made sweet pastry
butter, for greasing

filling

2 eggs
grated rind and juice of 2 lemons
200 g/7 oz golden caster sugar
375 ml/13 fl oz double cream
250 g/9 oz dessicated coconut

method

1 On a lightly floured work surface, roll out the pastry and use it to line a greased 23-cm/9-inch tart tin. Line with baking parchment and fill with baking beans, then bake in a preheated oven, 200°C/400°F, for 15 minutes. Remove the paper and beans and return to the oven for a further 5 minutes. Reduce the oven temperature to 160°C/325°F and place a baking sheet in the oven.

2 To make the filling, place the eggs, lemon rind and sugar in a bowl and beat together for 1 minute. Gently stir in the cream, then the lemon juice and finally the coconut.

3 Spoon the filling into the pastry case and place the tart tin on the preheated baking sheet. Bake for 40 minutes or until set and golden. Cool for 1 hour to firm up. Serve at room temperature.

caramelized lemon tart

ingredients

SERVES 6

pastry

100 g/3½ oz cold butter, cut into pieces, plus extra for greasing
200 g/7 oz plain flour
pinch of salt
2 tbsp caster sugar
1 egg yolk
cold water

filling

5 lemons
2 eggs
275 g/9½ oz caster sugar
175 g/6 oz ground almonds
125 ml/4 fl oz whipping cream
100 ml/3½ fl oz water

whipped cream, to serve

method

1 Lightly grease a 9-inch/22-cm loose-based fluted tart tin. Sift the flour and salt into a food processor, add the butter and process until the mixture resembles fine breadcrumbs. Tip the mixture into a large bowl, then add the sugar and egg yolk and just enough cold water to bring the pastry together. Roll out the pastry onto a lightly floured work surface to a circle 8 cm/3¼ inches larger than the tin. Lift the pastry carefully into the tin, press to fit and trim the excess pastry. Fit baking parchment into the pastry case and fill with baking beans. Chill in the refrigerator for 30 minutes, then bake for 10 minutes in a preheated oven, 190°C/375°F. Remove the beans and paper and bake for a further 5 minutes.

2 Put the juice and finely grated rind of 3 of the lemons in a bowl. Add the eggs, 85 g/3 oz of the sugar, the ground almonds and the cream, whisking to combine. Pour into the pastry case and bake for 25 minutes.

3 Thinly slice the remaining 2 lemons, discarding the seeds and ends. Heat the remaining sugar and water in a saucepan until the sugar is dissolved. Simmer for 5 minutes, then add the lemon slices and boil for 10 minutes. Arrange the lemon slices over the surface of the cooked tart in a spiral pattern. Drizzle over the remaining lemon syrup. Serve warm or cold, with whipped cream.

peach & preserved ginger tarte tatin

ingredients

SERVES 6

250 g/9 oz ready-made puff pastry
flour, for dusting

filling

6–8 just ripe peaches
100 g/3½ oz golden caster sugar
3 heaped tbsp unsalted butter
3 pieces preserved ginger in syrup, chopped
1 tbsp ginger syrup from the preserved ginger jar
1 egg, beaten

thick cream or ice cream, to serve

method

1 Plunge the peaches into boiling water, then drain and peel. Cut each in half. Put the sugar in a 25-cm/10-inch heavy, ovenproof frying pan and heat gently until it caramelizes. Don't stir, just shake the pan if necessary. Once the sugar turns a dark caramel colour, remove from the heat immediately and drop 2 tbsp of the butter into it.

2 Place the peaches cut-side up on top of the caramel, packing them as close together as possible and tucking the preserved ginger pieces into any gaps. Dot with the remaining butter and drizzle with the ginger syrup.

3 Return to gentle heat while you roll out the pastry in a circle larger than the frying pan you are using. Drape the pastry over the peaches and tuck it in well round the edges, brush with the beaten egg and bake in a preheated oven, 190°C/375°F, for 20–25 minutes or until the pastry is browned and puffed up. Remove from the oven and rest for 5 minutes, then invert on to a serving plate and serve with thick cream or ice cream.

walnut custard tarts

ingredients

SERVES 4

40 g/1$^{1}/_{2}$ oz butter

8 sheets filo pastry (work with one sheet at a time and keep the remaining sheets covered with a damp tea towel)

40 g/1$^{1}/_{2}$ oz walnut halves

150 g/5$^{1}/_{2}$ oz Greek yogurt

4 tbsp honey

150 ml/5 fl oz double cream

2 tbsp caster sugar

2 eggs

1 tsp vanilla essence

icing sugar, for dusting

Greek yogurt, to serve

method

1 Melt the butter. Brush 4 deep 10-cm/4-inch tartlet pans with a little of the butter. Cut the sheets of filo pastry in half to make 16 rough squares.

2 Take 1 square of pastry, brush it with a little of the melted butter and use it to line 1 of the pans. Repeat with 3 more pastry squares, placing each of them at a different angle. Line the remaining 3 pans and place the pans on a baking sheet.

3 To make the filling, finely chop 2 tablespoons of the walnuts. Put the yogurt, honey, cream, sugar, eggs and vanilla essence in a bowl and beat together. Stir in the chopped walnuts until well mixed.

4 Pour the yogurt filling into the pastry cases. Roughly break the remaining walnuts and scatter over the top. Bake in a preheated oven, 180°C/350°F, for 25–30 minutes until the filling is firm to the touch.

5 Cool the tartlets, then carefully remove from the pans and dust with icing sugar. Serve with a bowl of yogurt, if desired.

chocolate fudge tart

ingredients

SERVES 6–8

flour, for dusting
250 g/9 oz ready-made unsweetened pastry

filling

140 g/5 oz plain chocolate, finely chopped
175 g/6 oz butter, diced
250 g/9 oz golden granulated sugar
100 g/3½ oz plain flour
½ tsp vanilla essence
6 eggs, beaten

icing sugar, for dusting
150 ml/5 fl oz whipped cream and ground cinnamon, to decorate

method

1 Roll out the pastry on a lightly floured work surface and use to line a 20-cm/8-inch deep loose-based tart tin. Prick the pastry base lightly with a fork, then line with foil and fill with baking beans. Bake in a preheated oven, 200°C/400°F, for 12–15 minutes or until the pastry no longer looks raw. Remove the beans and foil and bake for 10 minutes more, or until the pastry is firm. Set aside to cool. Reduce the oven temperature to 180°C/350°F.

2 To make the filling, place the chocolate and butter in a heatproof bowl and melt over a saucepan of gently simmering water. Stir until smooth, then remove from the heat and set aside to cool. Place the sugar, flour, vanilla essence and eggs in a separate bowl and whisk until well blended. Stir in the butter and chocolate mixture.

3 Pour the filling into the pastry case and bake in the oven for 50 minutes or until the filling is just set. Transfer to a wire rack to cool completely. Dust with icing sugar before serving with whipped cream sprinkled lightly with cinnamon.

crème brûlée tarts

ingredients

SERVES 6

pastry

150 g/5½ oz plain flour, plus extra for dusting
1–2 tbsp caster sugar
125 g/4½ oz butter, cut into pieces
1 tbsp water

filling

4 egg yolks
50 g/1½ oz caster sugar
400 ml/14 fl oz double cream
1 tsp vanilla essence
raw brown sugar, for sprinkling

method

1 To make the pastry, place the flour and sugar in a large bowl. Rub in the butter with your fingertips until the mixture resembles breadcrumbs. Add the water and mix to form a soft dough. Wrap and chill for 30 minutes.

2 Divide the pastry into 6 pieces. Roll out each piece on a lightly floured work surface to line 6 x 10-cm/4-inch tart tins. Prick the bottom of the pastry with a fork and chill for 20 minutes.

3 Line the pastry cases with foil and baking beans and bake in a preheated oven, 190°C/ 375°F, for 15 minutes. Remove the foil and baking beans and cook the pastry cases for a further 10 minutes or until crisp. Set aside to cool.

4 To make the filling, beat the egg yolks and sugar together in a bowl until pale. Heat the cream and vanilla essence in a saucepan until just below boiling point, then pour it on to the egg mixture, whisking constantly. Return the mixture to a clean pan and bring to just below the boil, stirring, until thick. Do not allow the mixture to boil or it will curdle. Cool slightly, then pour it into the tart tins. Cool, then chill overnight.

5 Preheat the grill. Sprinkle the tarts with the sugar. Cook under the grill for a few minutes. Cool, then chill for 2 hours before serving.

summer fruit tartlets

ingredients

MAKES 12

pastry

200 g/7 oz plain flour, plus extra for dusting
85 g/3 oz icing sugar
55 g/2 oz ground almonds
115 g/4 oz butter
1 egg yolk
1 tbsp milk

filling

225 g/8 oz cream cheese
icing sugar, to taste, plus extra for dusting
250 g/9 oz fresh summer fruits, such as red and whitecurrants, blueberries, raspberries and small strawberries

method

1 To make the pastry, sift the flour and icing sugar into a bowl. Stir in the ground almonds. Add the butter and rub in until the mixture resembles breadcrumbs. Add the egg yolk and milk and work in with a spatula, then mix with your fingers until the pastry binds together. Wrap the pastry in clingfilm and chill in the refrigerator for 30 minutes.

2 On a floured work surface, roll out the pastry and use to line 12 deep tartlet or individual brioche pans. Prick the bottoms. Press a piece of foil into each tartlet, covering the edges and bake in a preheated oven, 200°C/400°F, for 10–15 minutes or until light golden brown. Remove the foil and bake for a further 2–3 minutes. Transfer to a wire rack to cool.

3 To make the filling, place the cream cheese and icing sugar in a bowl and mix together. Place a spoonful of filling in each pastry case and arrange the fruit on top. Dust with sifted icing sugar and serve.

full of fruit

In many cultures, the 'dessert' usually consists of nothing more than a selection of fresh, seasonal fruit. This, of course, has much to commend it, because all the essential vitamin content of the fruit is preserved when eaten this way – but when there are so many marvellous ways to turn a simple fruit into something a little different and truly delicious, it seems a shame not to experiment!

A great way to start is to take a selection of fresh fruits and serve them with a chocolate fondue – this really is the best of both worlds. In Mediterranean countries, where fruit grows in abundance, it is often poached or baked. The Spiced Apricots in Red Wine from France are very good – the cooking liquid is reduced to a thick, tasty syrup for pouring over the fruit – as are the Valencia Caramel Oranges from Spain and the Marsala Cherries from Italy. If you love fresh figs, try them grilled with honey and served with a frothy sabayon sauce – sprinkling the figs with a little chopped rosemary as you grill them is optional, but well worth doing.

Exotic fruits are given an unusual twist here. Try serving your favourite encased in a chocolate crèpe, or serve colourful Steamed Spiced Exotic Fruits in their own little 'bag'. And children will love Toffee Bananas, coated in crisp caramel and irresistible!

grilled honeyed figs with sabayon

ingredients

SERVES 4

8 fresh figs, cut in half
4 tbsp honey
2 fresh rosemary sprigs, leaves removed and finely chopped (optional)
3 eggs

method

1 Preheat the grill to high. Arrange the figs, cut-side up, on the grill pan. Brush with half the honey and sprinkle over the chopped rosemary, if using. Cook under the preheated grill for 5–6 minutes or until just starting to caramelize.

2 Meanwhile, to make the sabayon, lightly whisk the eggs in a large, heatproof bowl with the remaining honey, then place over a saucepan of simmering water. Using a hand-held electric whisk, beat the eggs and honey together for 10 minutes or until pale and thick.

3 Put 4 fig halves on each of 4 serving plates, add a generous spoonful of the sabayon and serve at once.

grilled bananas

ingredients

SERVES 4

55 g/2 oz block creamed coconut, chopped

150 ml/5 fl oz double cream

4 bananas

juice and rind of 1 lime

1 tbsp vegetable or peanut oil

50 g/1¾ oz dessicated coconut

method

1 Put the creamed coconut and cream in a small saucepan and heat gently until the coconut has dissolved. Remove from the heat and set aside to cool for 10 minutes, then whisk until thick but floppy.

2 Peel the bananas and toss in the lime juice and rind. Lightly oil a preheated grill pan and cook the bananas, turning once, for 2–3 minutes or until soft and browned.

3 Toast the dry unsweetened coconut on a piece of foil under the grill until lightly browned. Serve the bananas with the coconut cream, sprinkled with the toasted coconut.

toffee bananas

ingredients

SERVES 4

70 g/2½ oz self-raising flour
1 egg, beaten
5 tbsp iced water
4 large, ripe bananas
3 tbsp lemon juice
2 tbsp rice flour
vegetable oil, for deep-frying

caramel

115 g/4 oz caster sugar
4 tbsp iced water, plus an extra bowl of iced water for setting
2 tbsp sesame seeds

method

1 Sift the flour into a bowl. Make a well in the centre, add the egg and 5 tablespoons of the iced water and beat from the centre outwards, until combined into a smooth batter.

2 Peel the bananas and cut into 5-cm/2-inch pieces. Gently shape them into balls with your hands. Brush with lemon juice to prevent discoloration, then roll them in rice flour until coated. Pour oil into a saucepan to a depth of 6 cm/2½ inches and preheat to 190°C/375°F. Coat the balls in the batter and cook in batches in the hot oil for about 2 minutes each, until golden. Lift them out and drain on kitchen paper.

3 To make the caramel, put the sugar into a small saucepan over low heat. Add 4 tablespoons of iced water and heat, stirring, until the sugar dissolves. Simmer for 5 minutes, remove from the heat and stir in the sesame seeds. Toss the banana balls in the caramel, scoop them out and drop into the bowl of iced water to set. Lift them out and divide between individual serving bowls. Serve hot.

banana-stuffed crêpes

ingredients

SERVES 4

225 g/8 oz plain flour

2 tbsp soft light brown sugar

2 eggs

450 ml/15 fl oz milk

grated rind and juice of 1 lemon

55 g/2 oz butter

3 bananas

4 tbsp golden syrup

method

1 Combine the flour and sugar and beat in the eggs and half the milk. Beat together until smooth. Gradually add the remaining milk, stirring constantly to make a smooth batter. Stir in the lemon rind.

2 Melt a little butter in an 20-cm/8-inch frying pan and pour in a quarter of the batter. Tilt the pan to coat the bottom and cook for 1–2 minutes or until set. Flip the crêpe over and cook the second side. Slide out of the pan and keep warm. Repeat to make 3 more crêpes.

3 Slice the bananas and toss them in the lemon juice. Pour the syrup over them and toss together. Fold each crêpe in half and then in half again and fill the centre with the banana mixture. Serve warm.

baked stuffed honey figs

ingredients

SERVES 4

150 ml/5 fl oz fresh orange juice

6 tbsp honey

12 no-soak dried figs

40 g/1½ oz shelled pistachio nuts, chopped finely

25 g/1 oz no-soak dried apricots, chopped very finely

1 tsp sesame seeds

Greek yogurt, to serve

method

1 Put the orange juice and 5 tablespoons of the honey in a saucepan and heat gently to dissolve the honey. Add the figs and simmer for 10 minutes or until softened. Remove from the heat and cool in the liquid.

2 Meanwhile, prepare the filling. Put the nuts, apricots, sesame seeds and remaining tablespoon of honey in a bowl and mix well.

3 Using a slotted spoon, remove the figs from the cooking liquid and reserve. Cut a slit at the top of each fig, where the stem joins. Using your fingers, plump up the figs and stuff each one with about 1 teaspoon of the filling mixture. Close the top of each fig and place in an ovenproof dish. Pour over the reserved cooking liquid.

4 Bake the figs in a preheated oven, 170°C/325°F, for 10 minutes or until hot. Serve warm or cold, with the sauce and Greek yogurt.

baked stuffed peaches

ingredients

SERVES 4

- 4 ripe peaches
- 4 tbsp unsalted butter
- 2 tbsp soft brown sugar
- 55 g/2 oz crushed amaretti or macaroons
- 2 tbsp Amaretto liqueur
- 125 ml/4 fl oz single cream, to serve

method

1 Prepare the peaches by cutting them in half and removing the stones (if you want to peel them, just dip them into boiling water for 10–15 seconds and then plunge them into cold water). Place the peaches cut sides up in an ovenproof dish greased with 1 tablespoon of the butter.

2 In a bowl, combine the remaining butter and sugar until creamy, then add the amaretti or macaroons and mix well. Stuff the peaches with the biscuit filling.

3 Bake in the centre of a preheated oven, 180°C/350°F, for 20–25 minutes or until the peaches are soft. Pour over the liqueur and serve hot with the single cream.

peaches with raspberry sauce

ingredients

SERVES 4-6

450 g/1 lb fresh raspberries
finely grated rind of 1 orange
2 tbsp freshly squeezed orange juice
2 tbsp Grand Marnier, Cointreau, or other orange-flavoured liqueur
2–3 tbsp caster sugar
6 ripe fresh peaches
vanilla ice cream, to serve
langues de chats, to serve (optional)

method

1 Purée the raspberries in a food processor or blender, then press through a fine non-metallic sieve into a mixing bowl to remove the seeds.

2 Stir the orange rind and juice and liqueur into the raspberry purée. Add sugar to taste, stirring until the sugar dissolves. Cover and chill in the refrigerator until required.

3 Meanwhile, bring a large saucepan of water to the boil over high heat. Add the peaches, 1 or 2 at a time, and let them stand in the water for 10–20 seconds, then remove with a slotted spoon. When the peaches are cool enough to handle, peel off the skins, then cut them in half and remove the stones.

4 Cut each peach half into two and stir into the raspberry sauce. Cover and chill in the refrigerator until required.

5 When ready to serve, put a scoop or two of ice cream into individual glasses or bowls, then top with the peaches and spoon some extra sauce over. Serve with the langues de chats on the side, if using.

baked apricots with honey

ingredients

SERVES 4

butter, for greasing
4 apricots, each cut in half and pitted
4 tbsp flaked almonds
4 tbsp honey
pinch ground ginger or grated nutmeg
vanilla ice cream, to serve (optional)

method

1 Lightly butter an ovenproof dish large enough to hold the apricot halves in a single layer.

2 Arrange the apricot halves in the dish, cut sides up. Sprinkle with the almonds and drizzle the honey over. Dust with the spice.

3 Bake in a preheated oven, 200°C/400°F, for 12–15 minutes until the apricots are tender and the almonds golden. Remove from the oven and serve at once, with ice cream on the side, if desired.

spiced apricots in red wine

ingredients

SERVES 4–6

- 1/2 tsp white peppercorns, lightly crushed
- 3 cloves
- 350 ml/12 fl oz full-bodied red wine, such as Côtes du Rhône
- 200 ml/7 fl oz water
- 200 g/7 oz sugar
- 1-cm/1/2-inch piece of fresh root ginger, peeled and finely sliced
- 1 cinnamon stick
- 6 tender fresh apricots
- freshly grated nutmeg
- 2 tbsp toasted flaked almonds, to decorate
- crème fraîche, to serve (optional)

method

1 Place the peppercorns and cloves in a dry sauté pan or frying pan over high heat and toast, stirring constantly, for 1 minute, or until the aroma develops. Immediately tip them out of the pan. Place the peppercorns in a mortar and lightly crush with a pestle.

2 Put the wine, water, sugar, peppercorns, cloves, ginger and cinnamon stick in a heavy-based saucepan over high heat and stir to dissolve the sugar. When the sugar has dissolved, bring the liquid to the boil, without stirring, and boil for 8 minutes.

3 Add the apricots to the syrup, then reduce the heat to low and simmer for 5 minutes or until just tender when pierced with the tip of a knife. Use a slotted spoon to remove the apricots from the syrup and transfer to a bowl of iced water to cool. When the apricots are cool enough to handle, peel them, then cut them in half, remove the stones and transfer to a serving bowl.

4 Meanwhile, return the syrup to boiling point and boil until it becomes thick. Grate in the nutmeg to taste. Remove the syrup from the heat and let it cool, then pour it over the apricot halves. Cover and chill.

5 Serve the apricots with a generous portion of the syrup, the toasted flaked almonds and a dollop of crème fraîche on the side, if using.

oranges in caramel sauce

ingredients

SERVES 6

9 oranges

175 ml/6 fl oz water

250 g/9 oz white granulated sugar

3 tbsp Greek honey

method

1 Using a zester, remove the zest from the oranges and put in a small saucepan. Add the water and leave to soak for 1 hour.

2 When the orange zest has soaked, simmer for 20 minutes. Strain any remaining liquid, reserving the zest, into a measuring jug and add water to make up to 175 ml/6 fl oz again.

3 Using a sharp knife, remove the peel from the oranges, discarding all the white pith. Cut the flesh widthways into 1/2-cm/1/4-inch slices and arrange in a glass serving dish, scattered with a little of the orange zest. Reserve most of the zest to decorate.

4 Put the measured water and the sugar in a saucepan and heat until the sugar has dissolved, then bring to the boil and boil rapidly until it turns a pale golden colour. Immediately remove from the heat, stir in the honey until dissolved and then add the reserved orange zest. Cool slightly, then pour the caramel sauce over the oranges. Chill in the refrigerator for at least 3 hours before serving, decorated with the reserved zest.

valencia caramel oranges

ingredients

SERVES 4–6

4 large, juicy oranges

250 g/9 oz caster sugar

300 ml/10 fl oz water

4–6 tbsp flaked almonds, toasted, to serve

method

1 Working over a heatproof bowl to catch any juices and using a small serrated knife, pare the oranges, taking care not to leave any of the bitter-tasting pith. Use the knife to remove the orange segments, cutting between the membranes. Squeeze the empty membranes over the bowl to extract as much juice as possible; discard the membranes and set the segments and juice aside.

2 Put the sugar and 150 ml/5 fl oz of the water into a small, heavy-based saucepan over medium-high heat. Stir until the sugar dissolves, then bring to the boil and boil, without stirring, until the syrup turns a rich golden brown.

3 Pour the remaining water into the pan (stand back because the caramel will splatter). Stir again until the caramel dissolves. Remove from the heat and cool the caramel slightly, then pour over the oranges. Stir to blend the orange juice into the caramel. Cool the oranges completely, then cover with clingfilm and chill for at least 2 hours before serving.

4 Just before serving, sprinkle the caramel oranges with the toasted flaked almonds.

roasted spicy pineapple

ingredients

SERVES 4

1 pineapple
1 mango, peeled, stoned and sliced
55 g/2 oz butter
4 tbsp golden syrup
1–2 tsp cinnamon
1 tsp freshly grated nutmeg
4 tbsp soft brown sugar
2 passion fruit
150 ml/5 fl oz crème fraîche
finely grated rind of 1 orange

method

1 Use a sharp knife to cut off the top, base and skin of the pineapple, then cut into quarters. Remove the central core and cut the flesh into large cubes. Place them in a roasting tin with the mango.

2 Place the butter, syrup, cinnamon, nutmeg and sugar in a small saucepan and heat gently, stirring constantly, until melted. Pour the mixture over the fruit. Roast in a preheated oven, 200°C/400°F, for 20–30 minutes or until the fruit is browned.

3 Halve the passion fruit and scoop out the seeds. Spoon over the roasted fruit. Mix the crème fraîche and orange rind together and serve with the fruit.

pears in honey syrup

ingredients

SERVES 4

4 medium-ripe pears

200 ml/7 fl oz water

1 tsp sugar

1 tbsp honey

method

1 Peel each pear, leaving the stem intact. Wrap each pear in foil and place in a saucepan with the stems resting on the side of the pan. Add enough water to come at least half way up the pears. Bring to the boil and simmer for 30 minutes. Remove the pears and carefully remove the foil, reserving any juices. Set aside to cool.

2 Bring the measured water to the boil. Add any pear juices, the sugar and the honey and boil for 5 minutes. Remove from the heat and cool a little.

3 Place each pear in an individual dish. Pour a little syrup over each and serve just warm.

poached pears with chocolate sauce

ingredients

SERVES 4

4 ripe dessert pears, such as Conference
juice of 1/2 lemon
350 ml/12 fl oz Beaumes-de-Venise dessert wine
175 ml/6 fl oz water
1 vanilla pod, split
vanilla ice cream, to serve

chocolate sauce

175 g/6 oz plain chocolate, broken up
5 tbsp water
4 tbsp double cream

method

1 Peel and core the pears, then cut into quarters, dropping them into a bowl of water with the lemon juice squeezed in to prevent discoloration.

2 Put the wine, water and split vanilla pod in a sauté pan over high heat. Add the pear quarters and bring the liquid to the boil. As soon as it boils, reduce the heat until the point that small bubbles appear around the edge. Poach the pears for 5–10 minutes or until tender when pierced with the tip of a knife.

3 Use a slotted spoon to transfer the pear quarters to an ovenproof serving dish as they become tender. When all the pears are removed from the liquid, return the liquid to the boil and continue boiling until reduced to about 4 tablespoons. Pour the syrup and vanilla pod over the pears and cool completely. Cover the surface with clingfilm and chill for at least 1 hour or overnight.

4 Just before serving, make the chocolate sauce. Stir the chocolate and water in a small pan over low heat until melted and smooth. Remove from the heat and beat in the cream.

5 To serve, spoon a scoop of ice cream into individual serving bowls and add the poached pears. Spoon over the hot chocolate sauce.

marsala cherries

ingredients

SERVES 4

140 g/5 oz caster sugar
thinly pared rind of 1 lemon
5-cm/2-in piece of cinnamon stick
225 ml/8 fl oz water
225 ml/8 fl oz Marsala
900 g/2 lb Morello cherries, pitted
150 ml/5 fl oz double cream

method

1 Put the sugar, lemon rind, cinnamon stick, water and Marsala in a heavy-based saucepan and bring to the boil, stirring constantly. Reduce the heat and simmer for 5 minutes. Remove the cinnamon stick.

2 Add the Morello cherries, cover and simmer gently for 10 minutes. Using a slotted spoon, transfer the cherries to a bowl.

3 Return the pan to the heat and bring to the boil over high heat. Boil for 3–4 minutes or until thick and syrupy. Pour the syrup over the cherries and set aside to cool, then chill for at least 1 hour.

4 Whisk the cream until stiff peaks form. To serve, divide the cherries and syrup between 4 individual dishes or glasses and top with the whipped cream.

poached fruit, seville style

ingredients

SERVES 4–6

syrup

- 1/2 tsp fennel seeds
- 1/2 tsp coriander seeds
- 1/4 tsp black peppercorns
- 200 g/7 oz caster sugar
- 225 ml/8 fl oz red wine, such as Rioja
- 225 ml/8 fl oz water
- 3 tbsp freshly squeezed orange juice
- 2 tbsp freshly squeezed lemon juice
- 2 tbsp Spanish cream sherry
- 3 cloves
- 1 cinnamon stick
- 12 tender apricots, halved and pitted
- 2 tbsp flaked almonds, toasted, to decorate

method

1 To make the red wine syrup, put the fennel and coriander seeds and peppercorns in a heavy-based saucepan over high heat and dry-fry for up to about 1 minute until they start to give off an aroma. Immediately tip them out of the pan to stop the cooking. Put in a mortar and lightly crush.

2 Put the sugar, wine, water, orange and lemon juices, sherry and all the spices into a heavy-based saucepan over medium-high heat, stirring to dissolve the sugar. Bring to the boil and let bubble, without stirring, for 5 minutes. Add the fruit and simmer for 6–8 minutes until tender. Remove the pan from the heat, transfer to a bowl of iced water and cool. When cool enough to handle, remove the apricots and peel. Cover and chill until required.

3 Meanwhile, return the juices to the heat and boil until the syrup thickens and the flavours become more concentrated. Remove from the heat and cool.

4 To serve, place the fruit in serving bowls, spoon the syrup over, then sprinkle with flaked almonds.

warm fruit nests

ingredients

SERVES 4

2–3 tbsp lemon-infused olive oil
8 sheets of frozen filo pastry, thawed
250 g/9 oz blueberries
250 g/9 oz raspberries
250 g/9 oz blackberries
3 tbsp caster sugar
1 tsp ground allspice
sprigs of fresh mint, to decorate
double cream, to serve

method

1 Brush 4 small muffin tins with oil. Cut the filo pastry into 16 squares measuring about 12 cm/4½ inches across. Brush each square with oil and use to line the muffin tins. Place 4 sheets in each tin, staggering them so that the overhanging corners make a decorative star shape. Transfer to a baking sheet and bake in a preheated oven, 180°C/350°F, for 7–8 minutes or until golden. Remove from the oven and set aside.

2 Meanwhile, warm the fruit in a saucepan with the caster sugar and allspice over medium heat until simmering. Lower the heat and continue simmering, stirring, for 10 minutes. Remove from the heat and drain. Using a perforated spoon, divide the warm fruit between the tartlet cases. Garnish with sprigs of fresh mint and serve warm with double cream.

mixed fruit salad

ingredients

SERVES 4

- 1 papaya, halved, peeled and deseeded
- 2 bananas, sliced thickly
- 1 small pineapple, peeled, halved, cored and sliced
- 12 lychees, peeled if fresh
- 1 small melon, deseeded and cut into thin wedges
- 2 oranges
- grated rind and juice of 1 lime
- 2 tbsp caster sugar

method

1 Arrange the papaya, bananas, pineapple, lychees and melon on a serving platter. Cut off the rind and pith from the oranges. Cut the orange segments out from between the membranes and add to the fruit platter. Grate a small quantity of the discarded orange rind and add to the platter.

2 Combine the lime rind, juice and sugar. Pour over the salad and serve.

steamed spiced exotic fruits

ingredients

SERVES 4

2 kiwi fruit, peeled and halved
4 rambutan or lychees, peeled, halved and stoned
2 passion fruit, the flesh scooped out
8 Cape gooseberries (physalis), papery leaves removed and fruit halved
85 g/3 oz mango, cut into 2-cm/¾-inch cubes
1 sharon fruit, cut into 2-cm/¾-inch slices
85 g/3 oz fresh raspberries
2 vanilla pods, split in half lengthways
2 cinnamon sticks, broken in half
4 star anise
4 fresh bay leaves
4 tbsp freshly squeezed orange juice

method

1 Cut 4 x 40 x 40-cm/16 x 16-inch squares of baking parchment and 4 foil squares of the same size. Put each baking parchment square on top of a foil square and fold them diagonally in half to form a triangle. Open up again.

2 Divide the fruits into 4 and arrange each portion neatly in the centre of each opened square. Add a vanilla pod half, a cinnamon stick half, a star anise, a bay leaf and 1 tbsp orange juice to each triangle.

3 Close each triangle over the mixture, fold in the corners and crumple the edges together to form airtight triangular bags. Transfer the bags to a baking sheet and bake in a preheated oven, 200°C/400°F, for 10–12 minutes or until they puff up with steam.

4 To serve, put each bag on a serving plate and snip open at the table.

chocolate fondue

ingredients

SERVES 6

1 pineapple

1 mango

12 Cape gooseberries (physalis)

250 g/9 oz fresh strawberries

250 g/9 oz deseeded green grapes

fondue

250 g/9 oz plain chocolate, broken into pieces

150 ml/5 fl oz double cream

2 tbsp brandy

method

1 Using a sharp knife, peel and core the pineapple, then cut the flesh into cubes. Peel the mango and cut the flesh into cubes. Peel back the papery outer skin of the Cape gooseberries and twist at the top to make a 'handle'. Arrange all the fruit on 6 serving plates and chill in the refrigerator.

2 To make the fondue, place the chocolate and cream in a fondue pot. Heat gently, stirring constantly, until the chocolate has melted. Stir in the brandy until it is thoroughly blended and the chocolate mixture is smooth.

3 Place the fondue pot over the burner to keep warm. To serve, allow each guest to dip the fruit into the sauce, using fondue forks or bamboo skewers.

exotic fruit chocolate crêpes

ingredients

SERVES 4

100 g/3½ oz plain flour
2 tbsp cocoa powder
pinch of salt
1 egg, beaten
300 ml/10 fl oz milk
oil, for frying
icing sugar, for dusting

filling

100 g/3½ oz thick plain yogurt
250 g/9 oz Mascarpone cheese
icing sugar (optional)
1 mango, peeled and diced
225 g/8 oz strawberries, hulled and quartered
2 passion fruit

method

1 To make the filling, place the yogurt and Mascarpone cheese in a bowl and sweeten with icing sugar, if you like. Place the mango and strawberries in a bowl and mix together. Cut the passion fruit in half, scoop out the pulp and seeds and add to the mango and strawberries. Stir together, then set aside.

2 To make the crêpes, sift the flour, cocoa powder and salt into a bowl and make a well in the centre. Add the egg and whisk with a balloon whisk. Gradually beat in the milk, drawing in the flour from the sides, to make a smooth batter. Cover and stand for 20 minutes. Heat a small amount of oil in an 18-cm/7-inch crêpe pan or frying pan. Pour in just enough batter to coat the bottom of the pan thinly. Cook over medium-high heat for 1 minute, then turn and cook the other side for 30–60 seconds or until cooked through.

3 Transfer the crêpe to a plate and keep hot. Repeat with the remaining batter, stacking the cooked crêpes on top of each other with waxed paper in between. Keep warm in the oven while cooking the remainder. To serve, divide the filling between the crêpes, then roll up and dust with icing sugar.

pavlova

ingredients

SERVES 4

6 egg whites
pinch of cream of tartar
pinch of salt
275 g/9½ oz caster sugar
600 ml/1 pint double cream
1 tsp vanilla essence
2 kiwi fruits, peeled and sliced
250 g/9 oz strawberries, hulled and sliced
3 ripe peaches, sliced
1 ripe mango, peeled and sliced
2 tbsp orange liqueur, such as Cointreau
fresh mint leaves, to decorate

method

1 Line 3 baking sheets with baking paper, then draw a 22-cm/8½-inch circle in the centre of each one. Beat the egg whites into stiff peaks. Mix in the cream of tartar and salt. Gradually add 200 g/7 oz of the sugar. Beat for 2 minutes until glossy. Fill a piping bag with the meringue mixture and pipe enough to fill each circle, doming them slightly in the centre. Bake in a preheated oven, 110°C/225°F, for 3 hours. Remove from the oven and cool.

2 Whip together the cream and vanilla essence with the remaining sugar. Put the fruit into a separate bowl and stir in the liqueur. Put one meringue circle onto a plate, then spread over a third of the sugared cream. Spread over a third of the fruit, then top with a meringue circle. Spread over another third of cream, then another third of fruit. Top with the last meringue circle. Spread over the remaining cream, followed by the rest of the fruit. Decorate with mint leaves and serve.

chilled desserts

Chilled desserts are the perfect choice for a dinner party, because you make them in advance and then forget about them until it is time to serve them, cool and delicious, to your guests.

For a family meal or a midweek get-together, a Creamy Mango Brûlée is a quick version of the classic French dish. If you have more time to spare, and want to impress with a really sophisticated dessert, go for the real thing – Espresso Crème Brûlée, or the Spanish version, Catalan Burnt Cream. Two variations of an intriguing dish are Floating Islands – poached meringues 'floating' in a lake of custard and drizzled with caramel – and Oeufs à la Neige au Chocolat, fluffy clouds of meringue on a chocolate custard.

Tiramisù, invented in the 1970s, has become a 'modern classic' and, in addition to the now familiar recipe, there's a second recipe included here, with a twist – the coffee-soaked sponge and creamy Mascarpone are layered with fresh cherries.

Mascarpone cheese has a natural sweetness, lending itself to use in desserts – try the Mascarpone Creams, made with crushed Amaretti biscuits for a crunchy texture, or Chocolate Brandy Torte, definitely one for the grown-ups! And talking of brandy, try the Zucotto – you make it the day before serving and it's divine!

espresso crème brûlée

ingredients

MAKES 4

450 ml/16 fl oz double cream

1 tbsp instant espresso powder

4 large egg yolks

100 g/3½ oz caster sugar

2 tbsp coffee liqueur, such as Kahlùa

4 tbsp caster sugar, for glazing

method

1 Place the cream in a small saucepan over medium-high heat and heat until small bubbles appear around the edges. Mix in the espresso powder, stirring until it dissolves, then remove the pan from the heat and stand until completely cool.

2 Lightly beat the egg yolks in a bowl, then add the sugar and continue beating until thick and creamy. Reheat the cream over medium-high heat until small bubbles appear around the edges. Stir into the egg-yolk mixture, beating constantly. Stir in the coffee liqueur.

3 Divide the custard mixture between 4 shallow white porcelain dishes placed on a baking sheet. Bake the custards in a preheated oven, 110°C/225°F, for 35–40 minutes or until the custard is just 'trembling' when you shake the dishes.

4 Remove the custards from the oven and cool completely. Cover the surfaces with clingfilm and chill in the refrigerator for at least 4 hours, but ideally overnight.

5 Just before you are ready to serve, sprinkle the surface of each custard with the remaining sugar and caramelize with a kitchen blow-torch or put the dishes under a very hot preheated grill until the topping is golden and bubbling. Cool for a few minutes for the caramel to harden before serving.

catalan burnt cream

ingredients

SERVES 6

750 ml/24 fl oz whole milk
1 vanilla pod, split
thinly pared rind of 1/2 lemon
7 large egg yolks
200 g/7 oz caster sugar
3 tbsp cornflour

method

1 A day in advance of serving, pour the milk into a saucepan with the vanilla pod and lemon rind. Bring to the boil, then remove from the heat and infuse for 30 minutes.

2 Put the eggs and 100 g/3 1/2 oz sugar in a heatproof bowl that will fit over a saucepan without touching the bottom and beat until the sugar dissolves and the mixture is creamy.

3 Return the infused milk to the heat and bring to a simmer, then stir 4 tablespoons into the cornflour in a bowl until a smooth paste forms. Stir into the milk over medium-low heat for 1 minute. Strain the milk into the egg mixture and whisk until well blended.

4 Put the bowl over a saucepan of simmering water and stir the custard for 25–30 minutes until thick enough to coat the back of the spoon; the bowl must not touch the water or the eggs might scramble. Spoon the mixture into 6 x 10-cm/4-inch round cazuelas or flat white crème brûlée dishes. Cool completely, then cover and chill for at least 12 hours.

5 To serve, sprinkle the top of each with a thin layer of caster sugar. Use a kitchen blowtorch to caramelize the sugar. Let stand while the caramel hardens, then serve. The caramel will remain firm for about 1 hour at room temperature; do not return to the fridge or the caramel will 'melt'.

creamy mango brûlée

ingredients

SERVES 4

2 mangoes
250 g/9 oz Mascarpone cheese
200 ml/7 fl oz thick natural yogurt
1 tsp ground ginger
grated rind and juice of 1 lime
2 tbsp light brown sugar
8 tbsp raw brown sugar

method

1 Slice the mangoes on either side of the stone. Discard the stone and peel the fruit. Slice and then chop the fruit and divide it between 4 ramekins.

2 Beat the Mascarpone cheese with the yogurt. Fold in the ginger, lime rind and juice and light brown sugar. Divide the mixture between the ramekins and level off the tops. Chill for 2 hours.

3 Sprinkle 2 tablespoons of raw brown sugar over the top of each dish, covering the creamy mixture. Place under a hot grill for 2–3 minutes or until melted and browned. Cool completely, then chill in the refrigerator.

spanish caramel custard

ingredients

SERVES 6

500 ml/18 fl oz whole milk
$1/2$ orange with 2 long, thin pieces of rind removed
1 vanilla pod, split, or $1/2$ tsp vanilla essence
175 g/6 oz caster sugar
butter, for greasing the dish
3 large eggs, plus 2 large egg yolks

method

1 Pour the milk into a saucepan with the orange rind and vanilla pod or extract. Bring to the boil, then remove from the heat and stir in 85 g/3 oz of the sugar; set aside for at least 30 minutes to infuse.

2 Meanwhile, put the remaining sugar and 4 tablespoons of water in a saucepan over medium-high heat. Stir until the sugar dissolves, then boil without stirring until the caramel turns deep golden brown. Remove from the heat immediately and squeeze in a few drops of orange juice to stop the cooking. Pour into a lightly buttered 1-litre/1$1/2$-pint soufflé dish and swirl to cover the base. Set aside.

3 Return the pan of infused milk to the heat and bring to a simmer. Beat the whole eggs and egg yolks together in a heatproof bowl. Pour the warm milk into the eggs, whisking constantly. Strain into the soufflé dish.

4 Place the soufflé dish in a roasting tin and pour in enough boiling water to come halfway up the sides of the dish. Bake in a preheated oven, 160°C/325°F, for 75–90 minutes until set and a knife inserted in the centre comes out clean. Remove the soufflé dish from the roasting tin and set aside to cool completely. Cover and chill overnight. To serve, run a metal spatula round the soufflé, then invert onto a serving plate, shaking firmly to release.

floating islands

ingredients

SERVES 4–6

1 litre/1$^{3}/_{4}$ pints milk, plus a little extra if necessary to make up the custard
1 vanilla pod, split
150 g/5$^{1}/_{2}$ oz caster sugar
6 egg yolks
1$^{1}/_{2}$ tbsp water
squeeze of lemon juice

meringues

2 large egg whites
$^{1}/_{2}$ tsp cream of tartar
55 g/2 oz caster sugar
55 g/2 oz icing sugar

method

1 To make the meringues, whisk the egg whites until frothy. Beat in the cream of tartar and continue whisking until soft peaks form. Adding the caster sugar 1 tablespoon at a time, whisk until stiff peaks form. Sift the icing sugar over and beat until glossy.

2 Slowly bring the milk to simmering point over medium-high heat in a wide frying pan. With a large wet spoon, drop a quarter of the meringue mixture into the milk. Poach for 5 minutes and drain on a tea towel. Repeat to make 3 more meringues.

3 Strain the milk and measure $^{3}/_{4}$ litre/1 pint. Add the vanilla pod and bring to the boil in a saucepan over medium heat. Remove from the heat, cover and stand. Beat 100 g/3$^{1}/_{2}$ oz of the sugar in a bowl with the egg yolks until thick and creamy. Remove the vanilla pod, then pour a quarter of the milk into the egg mixture, beating constantly. Return to the saucepan and simmer, stirring, for 10 minutes. Cool, then pour into 4 bowls. Add the meringues. Cover and chill.

4 Just before serving, dissolve the remaining sugar, stirring, in the water over medium-high heat. Bring to the boil and let bubble without stirring until a dark golden brown. Remove from the heat and add the lemon juice. To serve, drizzle the caramel over the meringues.

oeufs à la neige au chocolat

ingredients

SERVES 6

600 ml/1 pint milk

1 tsp vanilla essence

175 g/6 oz caster sugar

2 egg whites

cocoa powder, for dusting

custard

4 tbsp caster sugar

3 tbsp cocoa powder

4 egg yolks

method

1 Place the milk, vanilla essence and 5 tablespoons of the sugar in a heavy-based saucepan and stir over low heat until the sugar has dissolved. Simmer gently.

2 Whisk the egg whites in a spotlessly clean, greasefree bowl until stiff peaks form. Whisk in 2 teaspoons of the remaining sugar and continue to whisk until glossy. Gently fold in the rest of the sugar.

3 Drop large spoonfuls of the meringue mixture onto the simmering milk mixture and cook, stirring once, for 4–5 minutes or until the meringues are firm. Remove with a slotted spoon and let drain on kitchen paper. Poach the remaining meringues in the same way, then set aside the milk mixture.

4 To make the custard, mix the sugar, cocoa and egg yolks in the top of a double boiler or in a heatproof bowl. Gradually whisk in the reserved milk mixture. Place over a saucepan of barely simmering water and cook for 5–10 minutes, whisking constantly, until thickened. Remove from the heat and cool slightly. Divide the chocolate custard between 6 serving glasses and top with the meringues. Cover and chill in the refrigerator for at least 2 hours. When ready to serve, dust the tops of the meringues with cocoa.

coffee panna cotta with chocolate sauce

ingredients

SERVES 6

oil, for brushing
600 ml/1 pint double cream
1 vanilla pod
55 g/2 oz golden caster sugar
2 tsp instant espresso coffee granules, dissolved in 4 tbsp water
2 tsp powdered gelatine
chocolate-covered coffee beans, to serve

chocolate sauce

150 ml/5 fl oz single cream
55 g/2 oz plain chocolate, melted

method

1 Lightly brush 6 x 5-fl oz/150-ml moulds with oil. Place the cream in a saucepan. Split the vanilla pod and scrape the black seeds into the cream. Add the vanilla pod and the sugar, then heat gently until almost boiling. Sieve the cream into a heatproof bowl and reserve. Place the coffee in a small heatproof bowl, sprinkle on the gelatine and leave for 5 minutes or until spongy. Set the bowl over a saucepan of gently simmering water until the gelatine has dissolved.

2 Stir a little of the reserved cream into the gelatine mixture, then stir the gelatine mixture into the remainder of the cream. Divide the mixture between the prepared moulds and cool, then chill in the refrigerator for 8 hours, or overnight.

3 To make the sauce, place a quarter of the cream in a bowl and stir in the melted chocolate. Gradually stir in the remaining cream, reserving 1 tablespoon. To serve the panna cotta, dip the base of the moulds briefly into hot water and turn out onto 6 dessert plates. Pour the chocolate cream around. Dot drops of the reserved cream onto the sauce and feather it with a skewer. Decorate with chocolate-covered coffee beans and serve.

chocolate coeurs à la crème

ingredients

SERVES 8

225 g/8 oz ricotta cheese
55 g/2 oz icing sugar, sifted
300 ml/10 fl oz double cream
1 tsp vanilla essence
55 g/2 oz plain chocolate, grated
2 egg whites

coulis

225 g/8 oz fresh raspberries
icing sugar, to taste

to decorate

fresh strawberries, halved
fresh raspberries

method

1 Line 8 individual moulds with cheesecloth. Press the ricotta cheese through a sieve into a bowl. Add the icing sugar, cream and vanilla essence and beat together thoroughly. Stir in the grated chocolate. Place the egg whites in a separate clean bowl and whisk until stiff but not dry. Gently fold into the cheese mixture.

2 Spoon the mixture into the prepared moulds. Stand the moulds on a tray or dish and let them drain in the refrigerator for 8 hours, or overnight – the cheesecloth will absorb most of the liquid.

3 To make the raspberry coulis, place the raspberries in a food processor and process to a purée. Press the purée through a sieve into a bowl and add icing sugar, to taste. To serve, turn each dessert out onto a serving plate and pour the raspberry coulis round it. Decorate with strawberries and raspberries, then serve.

mascarpone creams

ingredients

SERVES 4

115 g/4 oz Amaretti biscuits, crushed

4 tbsp Amaretto or Maraschino

4 eggs, separated

55 g/2 oz caster sugar

225 g/8 oz Mascarpone cheese

toasted flaked almonds, to decorate

method

1 Place the Amaretti crumbs in a bowl, add the Amaretto or Maraschino and soak.

2 Meanwhile, beat the egg yolks with the caster sugar until pale and thick. Fold in the Mascarpone and soaked biscuit crumbs.

3 Whisk the egg white in a separate, spotlessly clean bowl until stiff, then gently fold into the cheese mixture. Divide the Mascarpone cream among 4 serving dishes and chill for 1–2 hours. Sprinkle with toasted flaked almonds just before serving.

chocolate rum creams

ingredients

SERVES 6

100 g/3½ oz plain chocolate, broken into pieces
150 ml/5 fl oz single cream
300 ml/10 fl oz whipping cream
1 tbsp icing sugar, sifted
2 tbsp white rum
chocolate curls, to decorate

method

1 Place the chocolate and single cream in a small, heavy-based saucepan and heat very gently until the chocolate has melted. Stir until smooth, then remove from the heat and cool. Pour the whipping cream into a large bowl and, using an electric whisk, whip until thick but not stiff.

2 Carefully whisk the sugar, rum and cooled chocolate mixture into the whipped cream. Take care not to overwhisk.

3 Spoon the mixture into 6 serving dishes or glasses, cover with clingfilm and chill in the refrigerator for 1–2 hours. Sprinkle chocolate curls carefully over the creams before serving.

chocolate mousse

ingredients

SERVES 4–6

225 g/8 oz plain chocolate, chopped
2 tbsp brandy, Grand Marnier or Cointreau
4 tbsp water
1 oz/30 g unsalted butter, diced
3 large eggs, separated
1/4 tsp cream of tartar
55 g/2 oz sugar
125 ml/4 fl oz double cream

method

1 Place the chocolate, brandy and water in a small saucepan over low heat and melt, stirring, until smooth. Remove the pan from the heat and beat in the butter. Beat the egg yolks into the chocolate mixture, one after another, until blended, then cool slightly.

2 Meanwhile, using an electric mixer on low speed, beat the egg whites in a spotlessly clean bowl until frothy, then gradually increase the mixer's speed and beat until soft peaks form. Sprinkle the cream of tartar over the surface, then add the sugar, tablespoon by tablespoon and continue beating until stiff peaks form. Beat several tablespoons of the egg whites into the chocolate mixture to loosen.

3 In another bowl, whip the cream until soft peaks form. Spoon the cream over the chocolate mixture, then spoon the remaining whites over the cream. Use a large metal spoon or rubber spatula to fold the chocolate into the cream and egg whites.

4 Either spoon the chocolate mousse into a large serving bowl or divide between 4 or 6 individual bowls. Cover the bowl(s) with clingfilm and chill the mousse for at least 3 hours before serving.

white chocolate mousse

ingredients

SERVES 6

250 g/9 oz white chocolate, broken into pieces
100 ml/3½ fl oz milk
300 ml/10 fl oz double cream
1 tsp rose water
2 egg whites
115 g/4 oz plain chocolate, broken into pieces
candied rose petals, to decorate

method

1 Place the white chocolate and milk in a saucepan and heat gently until the chocolate has melted, then stir. Transfer to a large bowl and cool.

2 Whip the cream and rose water in a separate bowl until soft peaks form. Whisk the egg whites in a separate large, spotlessly clean, greasefree bowl until stiff but not dry. Gently fold the whipped cream into the chocolate, then fold in the egg whites. Spoon the mixture into 6 small dishes or glasses, cover with clingfilm and chill for 8 hours, or overnight, to set.

3 Melt the plain chocolate and cool, then pour evenly over the mousses. Set aside until the chocolate has hardened, then decorate with rose petals and serve.

chestnut & chocolate terrine

ingredients

SERVES 6

200 ml/7 fl oz double cream
115 g/4 oz plain chocolate, melted and cooled
100 ml/3½ fl oz rum
1 package rectangular, plain, sweet biscuits
225 g/8 oz canned sweetened chestnut purée
cocoa powder, for dusting
icing sugar, to decorate

method

1 Line a 450-g/1-lb loaf tin with clingfilm. Place the cream in a bowl and whip lightly until soft peaks form. Using a spatula, fold in the cooled chocolate.

2 Place the rum in a shallow dish. Lightly dip 4 biscuits into the rum and arrange on the bottom of the tin. Repeat with 4 more biscuits. Spread half the chocolate cream over the biscuits. Make another layer of 8 biscuits dipped in rum and spread over the chestnut purée, followed by another layer of biscuits. Spread over the remaining chocolate cream and top with a final layer of biscuits. Cover with clingfilm and chill for 8 hours, or preferably overnight.

3 Turn the terrine out on to a large serving dish. Dust with cocoa powder. Cut strips of paper and place these randomly on top of the terrine. Sift over icing sugar, then carefully remove the paper. To serve, dip a sharp knife in hot water, dry it and use to cut the terrine into slices.

zucotto

ingredients

SERVES 6

115 g/4 oz soft margarine, plus extra for greasing
100 g/3½ oz self-raising flour
2 tbsp cocoa powder
½ tsp baking powder
115 g/4 oz golden caster sugar
2 eggs, beaten
3 tbsp brandy
2 tbsp Kirsch

filling

300 ml/10 fl oz double cream
25 g/1 oz icing sugar, sifted
55 g/2 oz toasted almonds, chopped
225 g/8 oz black cherries, pitted
55 g/2 oz plain chocolate, finely chopped

to decorate

1 tbsp cocoa powder
1 tbsp icing sugar
fresh cherries

method

1 Grease a 30 x 23-cm/12 x 9-inch Swiss roll tin and line it with baking parchment. Sift the flour, cocoa and baking powder into a bowl. Add the sugar, margarine and eggs. Beat together until well mixed, then spoon into the prepared tin. Bake in a preheated oven, 190°C/375°F, for 15–20 minutes or until well risen and firm to the touch. Let it stand in the tin for 5 minutes, then turn out onto a wire rack to cool.

2 Using the rim of a 1.2-litre/2½-pint ovenproof bowl as a guide, cut a circle from the cake and set aside. Line the bowl with clingfilm. Use the remaining cake, cutting it as necessary, to line the bowl. Place the brandy and Kirsch in a small bowl and mix together. Sprinkle over the cake, including the reserved circle.

3 To make the filling, pour the cream into a separate bowl and add the icing sugar. Whip until thick, then fold in the almonds, cherries and chocolate. Fill the sponge mould with the cream mixture and press the cake circle on top. Cover with a plate and a weight and chill in the refrigerator for 6–8 hours, or overnight. When ready to serve, turn the zucotto out onto a serving plate. Decorate with cocoa and icing sugar, sifted over in alternating segments and a few cherries.

chocolate trifle

ingredients

SERVES 4

280 g/10 oz ready-made chocolate loaf cake
3–4 tbsp seeded raspberry jam
4 tbsp Amaretto liqueur
250 g/9 oz package frozen mixed red fruit, thawed

custard

6 egg yolks
55 g/2 oz golden caster sugar
1 tbsp cornflour
500 ml/18 fl oz milk
55 g/2 oz plain chocolate, melted

topping

225 ml/8 fl oz double cream
1 tbsp golden caster sugar
1/2 tsp vanilla essence

to decorate

ready-made chocolate truffles
fresh fruit, such as cherries and strawberries

method

1 Cut the cake into slices and make 'sandwiches' with the raspberry jam. Cut the sandwiches into cubes and place in a large serving bowl. Sprinkle with the Amaretto liqueur. Spread the fruit over the cake.

2 To make the custard, place the egg yolks and sugar in a heatproof bowl and whisk until thick and pale, then stir in the cornflour. Place the milk in a saucepan and heat until almost boiling. Pour onto the egg yolk mixture, stirring. Return the mixture to the pan and bring just to the boil, stirring constantly, until it thickens. Remove from the heat and cool slightly. Stir in the melted chocolate. Pour the custard over the cake and fruit. Cool, then cover and chill in the refrigerator for 2 hours, or until set.

3 To make the topping, whip the cream until soft peaks form, then beat in the sugar and vanilla essence. Spoon over the trifle. Decorate with the truffles and fruit and chill until ready to serve.

tiramisù

ingredients

SERVES 4

- 200 ml/7 fl oz strong black coffee, cooled to room temperature
- 4 tbsp orange liqueur, such as Cointreau
- 3 tbsp orange juice
- 16 sponge fingers
- 250 g/9 oz Mascarpone cheese
- 300 ml/10 fl oz double cream, lightly whipped
- 3 tbsp icing sugar
- grated rind of 1 orange
- $2^1/_4$ oz/60 g plain chocolate, grated

to decorate

- chopped toasted almonds
- crystallized orange peel
- chocolate shavings

method

1 Pour the cooled coffee into a jug and stir in the orange liqueur and orange juice. Place 8 of the sponge fingers in the bottom of a serving dish, then pour over half of the coffee mixture.

2 Place the Mascarpone cheese in a separate bowl together with the cream, icing sugar and orange rind and mix well. Spread half of the Mascarpone mixture over the coffee-soaked sponge fingers, then arrange the remaining sponge fingers on top. Pour over the remaining coffee mixture then spread over the remaining Mascarpone mixture. Sprinkle over the grated chocolate and chill in the refrigerator for at least 2 hours.

3 Serve decorated with the chopped toasted almonds, crystallized orange peel and chocolate shavings.

cherry & chocolate tiramisù

ingredients

SERVES 4

200 ml/7 fl oz strong black coffee, cooled to room temperature
6 tbsp cherry brandy
16 trifle sponges
250 g/9 oz Mascarpone cheese
300 ml/10 fl oz double cream, lightly whipped
3 tbsp icing sugar
275 g/9½ oz sweet cherries, halved and pitted
60 g/2¼ oz chocolate, curls or grated
whole cherries, to decorate

method

1 Pour the cooled coffee into a jug and stir in the cherry brandy. Put half of the trifle sponges into the bottom of a serving dish, then pour over half of the coffee mixture.

2 Put the Mascarpone into a separate bowl along with the cream and sugar and mix well. Spread half of the Mascarpone mixture over the coffee-soaked trifle sponges, then top with half of the cherries. Arrange the remaining trifle sponges on top. Pour over the remaining coffee mixture and top with the remaining cherries. Finish with a layer of Mascarpone mixture. Scatter over the grated chocolate, cover with clingfilm and chill in the refrigerator for at least 2 hours.

3 Remove from the refrigerator, decorate with cherries and serve.

chocolate brandy torte

ingredients

SERVES 12

base

100 g/3½ oz butter, plus extra for greasing
250 g/9 oz ginger snaps
75 g/2¾ oz plain chocolate

filling

225 g/8 oz plain chocolate
250 g/9 oz Mascarpone cheese
2 eggs, separated
3 tbsp brandy
300 ml/10 fl oz double cream
4 tbsp caster sugar

to decorate

100 ml/3½ fl oz double cream
chocolate-covered coffee beans

method

1 Grease the bottom and sides of a 23-cm/9-inch springform cake tin. Place the gingersnaps in a plastic bag and crush with a rolling pin. Transfer to a bowl. Place the chocolate and butter in a small pan and heat gently until melted, then pour over the biscuits. Mix well, then press into the prepared tin. Chill while preparing the filling.

2 To make the filling, place the chocolate in a heatproof bowl set over a saucepan of simmering water and heat, stirring, until melted. Remove from the heat and beat in the Mascarpone cheese, egg yolks and brandy.

3 Whip the cream until just holding its shape. Fold in the chocolate mixture.

4 Whisk the egg whites in a spotlessly clean, greasefree bowl until soft peaks form. Add the sugar, a little at a time, and whisk until thick and glossy. Fold into the chocolate mixture, in 2 batches, until just mixed.

5 Spoon the mixture into the prepared base and chill in the refrigerator for at least 2 hours. Carefully transfer to a serving plate. To decorate, whip the cream and pipe onto the cheesecake, add the chocolate-covered coffee beans and serve.

manhattan cheesecake

ingredients

SERVES 8–10

6 tbsp butter
200 g/7 oz digestive biscuits, crushed
sunflower oil, for brushing
400 g/14 oz cream cheese
2 large eggs
140 g/5 oz caster sugar
$1^1/_2$ tsp vanilla essence
450 ml/16 fl oz sour cream

blueberry topping

55 g/2 oz caster sugar
4 tbsp water
250 g/9 oz fresh blueberries
1 tsp arrowroot

method

1 Melt the butter in a pan over low heat. Stir in the biscuits, then spread in a 20-cm/8-inch springform tin brushed with oil. Place the cream cheese, eggs, 100 g/$3^1/_2$ oz of the sugar and $^1/_2$ teaspoon of the vanilla essence in a food processor. Process until smooth. Pour over the biscuit base and smooth the top. Place on a baking sheet and bake in a preheated oven, 190°C/375°F, for 20 minutes until set. Remove from the oven and set aside for 20 minutes. Leave the oven switched on.

2 Mix the sour cream with the remaining sugar and vanilla essence in a bowl. Spoon over the cheesecake. Return it to the oven for 10 minutes, cool, then chill in the refrigerator for 8 hours or overnight.

3 To make the topping, place the sugar in a pan with 2 tablespoons of the water over low heat and stir until the sugar has dissolved. Increase the heat, add the blueberries, cover and cook for a few minutes or until they begin to soften. Remove from the heat. Mix the arrowroot and remaining water in a bowl, add to the fruit and stir until smooth. Return to low heat. Cook until the juice thickens and turns translucent, then set aside to cool.

4 Remove the cheesecake from the tin 1 hour before serving. Spoon the fruit topping over and chill until ready to serve.

irish cream cheesecake

ingredients

SERVES 12

oil, for brushing
175 g/6 oz chocolate chip cookies
55 g/2 oz butter

filling

225 g/8 oz plain chocolate
225 g/8 oz g milk chocolate
55 g/2 oz golden caster sugar
250 g/9 oz cream cheese
425 ml/15 fl oz double cream, whipped
3 tbsp Irish cream liqueur
crème fraîche or sour cream
fresh fruit, to serve

method

1 Line the base of a 20-cm/8-inch springform tin with foil and brush the sides with oil. Place the biscuits in a polythene bag and crush with a rolling pin. Place the butter in a saucepan and heat gently until just melted, then stir in the crushed biscuits. Press the mixture into the base of the tin and chill in the refrigerator for 1 hour.

2 To make the filling, melt the plain and milk chocolate together, stir to combine and leave to cool. Place the sugar and cream cheese in a large bowl and beat together until smooth, then fold in the whipped cream. Fold the mixture gently into the melted chocolate, then stir in the Irish cream liqueur.

3 Spoon the filling over the chilled biscuit base and smooth the surface. Cover and chill in the refrigerator for 2 hours, or until quite firm. Transfer to a serving plate and cut into small slices. Serve with a spoonful of crème fraîche and fresh fruit.

rice pudding

ingredients

SERVES 4–6

1 large orange

1 lemon

1 litre/$1^3/_4$ pints milk

250 g/9 oz Spanish short-grain rice

100 g/$3^1/_2$ oz caster sugar

1 vanilla pod, split

pinch of salt

125 ml/4 fl oz double cream

brown sugar, to serve (optional)

method

1 Finely grate the rinds from the orange and lemon and set aside. Rinse a heavy-based saucepan with cold water and do not dry it.

2 Put the milk and rice in the pan over medium-high heat and bring to the boil. Reduce the heat and stir in the caster sugar, vanilla pod, orange and lemon rinds and salt and simmer, stirring frequently, until the pudding is thick and creamy and the rice grains are tender: this can take up to 30 minutes, depending on how wide the pan is.

3 Remove the vanilla pod and stir in the cream. Serve at once, sprinkled with brown sugar, if desired, or cool completely, cover and chill until required. (The pudding will thicken as it cools, so stir in a little extra milk if necessary.)

summer pudding

ingredients

SERVES 6

675 g/1 lb 8 oz mixed summer berries, such as redcurrants, blackcurrants, raspberries and blackberries
140 g/5 oz caster sugar
2 tbsp crème de framboise liqueur (optional)
6–8 slices of good day-old white bread, crusts removed
double cream, to serve

method

1 Place the fruits in a large saucepan with the sugar. Over a low heat, very slowly bring to the boil, stirring carefully to ensure that the sugar has dissolved. Cook over low heat for only 2–3 minutes until the juices run but the fruit still holds its shape. Add the liqueur if using.

2 Line a 850-ml/1 1/2-pint pudding bowl with some of the slices of bread (cut them to shape so that the bread fits well). Spoon in the cooked fruit and juices, setting aside a little of the juice for later.

3 Cover the fruit with the remaining bread. Place a plate on top of the pudding and weight it down for at least 8 hours or overnight in the refrigerator.

4 Turn out the pudding and pour over the reserved juices to colour any white bits of bread that might be showing. Serve with the double cream.

ice creams

& sorbets

Ice creams and sorbets are so special that you might be forgiven for thinking there is some magic and mystery to their creation! In fact, they are surprisingly easy to make.

When making ice creams and sorbets, it is useful, but by no means essential, to have an ice cream maker. You simply prepare the mixture and pop it into the machine, following the manufacturer's instructions and keeping an eye on the recipe in case you need to add extra ingredients during the freezing process. Don't worry, however, if you don't have an ice cream maker – you can simply transfer the prepared mixture into a shallow freezerproof container and freeze for 2 hours, or until it is beginning to freeze around the edges. At this point, beat it well with a fork, then return it to the freezer until frozen. Transfer it from the freezer to the refrigerator about 30 minutes before you plan to serve it, to soften a little.

Armed with the tools for making a frozen dessert, the choice is now yours! There are one or two very simple recipes here – Banana and Coconut Ice Cream and Marshmallow Ice Cream take only moments to prepare and are easy to freeze – but it's worth mastering the art of making a simple sorbet and a vanilla custard ice cream, because once you've done that, the list of variations is almost endless!

cappuccino ice cream

ingredients

SERVES 4

150 ml/5 fl oz whole milk
600 ml/1 pint whipping cream
4 tbsp finely ground fresh coffee
3 large egg yolks
100 g/3½ oz caster sugar
cocoa powder, for dusting
chocolate-coated coffee beans, to decorate

method

1 Pour the milk and 450 ml/15 fl oz of the cream into a heavy-based saucepan, stir in the coffee and bring almost to the boil. Remove from the heat, infuse for 5 minutes, then strain through a paper filter or a sieve lined with cheesecloth.

2 Put the egg yolks and sugar in a large bowl and whisk together until pale and the mixture leaves a trail when the whisk is lifted. Slowly add the milk mixture, stirring all the time with a wooden spoon. Strain the mixture into the rinsed-out pan or a double boiler and cook over low heat for 10–15 minutes, stirring all the time, until the mixture thickens enough to coat the back of the spoon. Do not let the mixture boil or it will curdle. Remove from the heat and cool for at least 1 hour, stirring from time to time to prevent a skin forming.

3 Churn the cold custard in an ice cream maker, following the manufacturer's instructions.

4 To serve, whip the remaining cream until it holds its shape. Scoop the ice cream into wide-brimmed coffee cups and smooth the tops. Spoon the whipped cream over the top of each and sprinkle with cocoa powder. Decorate with chocolate-coated coffee beans.

rich vanilla ice cream

ingredients

SERVES 4–6

300 ml/10 fl oz single cream and 300 ml/10 fl oz double cream or 600 ml/1 pint whipping cream

1 vanilla pod

4 large egg yolks

100 g/3½ oz caster sugar

method

1 Pour the single and double cream or whipping cream into a large heavy-based saucepan. Split open the vanilla pod and scrape out the seeds into the cream, then add the whole vanilla pod, too. Bring almost to the boil, then remove from the heat and infuse for 30 minutes.

2 Put the egg yolks and sugar in a large bowl and whisk together until pale and the mixture leaves a trail when the whisk is lifted. Remove the vanilla pod from the cream, then slowly add the cream to the egg mixture, stirring all the time with a wooden spoon. Strain the mixture into the rinsed-out pan or a double boiler and cook over low heat for 10–15 minutes, stirring all the time, until the mixture thickens enough to coat the back of the spoon. Do not let the mixture boil or it will curdle. Remove from the heat and cool for at least 1 hour, stirring from time to time to prevent a skin forming.

3 Churn the custard in an ice cream maker, following the manufacturer's instructions. Serve immediately if wished, or transfer to a freezerproof container, cover with a lid and store in the freezer.

dairy strawberry ice cream

ingredients

SERVES 6

225 g/8 oz caster sugar
150 ml/5 fl oz water
900 g/2 lb fresh strawberries, plus extra to decorate
juice of 1/2 lemon
juice of 1/2 orange
300 ml/10 fl oz whipping cream

method

1 Put the sugar and water in a heavy-based saucepan and heat gently, stirring, until the sugar has dissolved. Bring to the boil, then boil for 5 minutes, without stirring, to form a syrup. Towards the end of the cooking time, keep an eye on the mixture to ensure that it does not burn. Immediately remove the syrup from the heat and cool for at least 1 hour.

2 Meanwhile, push the strawberries through a nylon sieve into a bowl to form a purée. When the syrup is cold, add the strawberry purée to it with the lemon juice and orange juice and stir well together. Whip the cream until it holds its shape. Keep in the refrigerator until ready to use.

3 If using an ice cream maker, fold the strawberry mixture into the whipped cream, then churn in the machine, following the manufacturer's instructions. Alternatively, freeze the mixture in a freezerproof container, uncovered, for 1–2 hours or until it starts to set around the edges. Turn the mixture into a bowl and stir with a fork or beat in a food processor until smooth. Fold in the whipped cream. Return to the freezer and freeze for a further 2–3 hours or until firm. Cover the container with a lid for storing. Serve decorated with strawberries.

rippled blackcurrant ice cream

ingredients

SERVES 6–8

425 ml/15 fl oz whole milk
1 vanilla pod
250 g/9 oz caster sugar
4 egg yolks
225 g/8 oz fresh blackcurrants, stripped from their stalks, plus extra to decorate
6 tbsp water
425 ml/15 fl oz whipping cream

method

1 Pour the milk into a saucepan, add the vanilla pod and bring almost to the boil. Infuse for 30 minutes, then remove the vanilla pod.

2 Put 115 g/4 oz of the sugar and the egg yolks in a large bowl and whisk until pale and the mixture leaves a trail when the whisk is lifted. Slowly add the milk, stirring constantly with a wooden spoon. Strain the mixture into a clean pan and cook over low heat for 10–15 minutes, stirring, until the mixture coats the back of the spoon. Do not let the custard boil. Remove from the heat and cool for at least 1 hour, stirring occasionally.

3 Put the blackcurrants in a heavy-based saucepan with the remaining sugar and the water. Heat gently, stirring, to dissolve the sugar, then simmer gently for 10 minutes or until the blackcurrants are very soft. Push through a nylon sieve into a bowl to remove the seeds, then let the purée cool.

4 Whip the cream until it holds its shape. Fold the custard into the cream, then churn in an ice cream maker. Just before the ice cream freezes, spread half in a freezerproof container. Pour over half the blackcurrant purée, then repeat the layers. Freeze for 1–2 hours or until firm. Serve decorated with blackcurrants.

lemon yogurt ice cream

ingredients

SERVES 4–6

2–3 lemons

600 ml/1 pint carton thick plain yogurt

150 ml/5 fl oz double cream

100 g/3½ oz caster sugar

finely pared lemon rind, to decorate

method

1 Squeeze the juice from the lemons – you need 6 tablespoons in total. Put the juice into a bowl, add the yogurt, cream and sugar and mix well together.

2 If using an ice cream maker, churn the mixture in the machine following the manufacturer's instructions. Alternatively, freeze the mixture in a freezerproof container, uncovered, for 1–2 hours or until it starts to set around the edges. Turn the mixture into a bowl and stir with a fork or beat in a food processor until smooth. Return to the freezer and freeze for a further 2–3 hours or until firm. Cover the container with a lid for storing. Serve with finely pared lemon rind.

blood orange ice cream

ingredients

SERVES 4–6

3 large blood oranges, washed
85 ml/3 fl oz semi-skimmed milk
85 ml/3 fl oz single cream
125 g/4½ oz caster sugar
4 large egg yolks
450 ml/16 fl oz double cream
⅛ tsp vanilla essence

method

1 Thinly pare the rind from 2 of the oranges, reserving a few strips for decoration, and finely grate the rind from the third. Squeeze the oranges to give 125 ml/4 fl oz juice and set aside.

2 Pour the milk and cream into a saucepan with the pared orange rind. Bring to the boil, then remove from the heat; set aside to infuse for at least 30 minutes.

3 Put the sugar and egg yolks in a heatproof bowl that fits over the pan without touching the bottom and beat until thick and creamy.

4 Return the milk mixture to the heat and bring to a simmer. Pour the milk onto the eggs and whisk until well blended. Rinse the pan, leaving a small amount of water in the bottom. Place over medium heat and bring the water to a simmer. Reduce the heat. Put the bowl on top and stir for about 20 minutes until a thick custard forms that coats the back of the spoon; the water must not touch the bottom of the bowl or the eggs might scramble.

5 Strain the mixture into a clean bowl. Stir in the finely grated orange rind and set aside for 10 minutes. Stir in the reserved juice, double cream and vanilla essence. Transfer to an ice cream maker and freeze, following the manufacturer's instructions. Decorate with strips of the reserved rind.

banana ice cream

ingredients

SERVES 8

3 bananas

2 tbsp lemon juice

1 tbsp white rum (optional)

200 g/7 oz icing sugar

600 ml/1 pint whipping cream

method

1 Peel and slice the bananas, then put the flesh in a food processor or blender. Add the lemon juice and process to form a very smooth purée. Turn the mixture into a large bowl. Alternatively, sprinkle the lemon juice over the banana slices, then push the flesh through a nylon sieve to form a purée. Add the rum, if using, and mix well together.

2 Sift the icing sugar into the mixture and beat until well mixed. Whip the cream until it holds its shape. Keep in the refrigerator until ready to use.

3 If using an ice cream maker, fold the whipped cream into the banana mixture, then churn the mixture in the machine following the manufacturer's instructions. Alternatively, freeze the mixture in a freezerproof container, uncovered, for 1–2 hours, or until it starts to set around the edges. Turn the mixture into a bowl and stir with a fork or beat in a food processor until smooth. Fold in the whipped cream. Return to the freezer and freeze for a further 2–3 hours, or until firm or required. Cover the container with a lid for storing.

banana & coconut ice cream

ingredients

SERVES 6–8

85 g/3 oz block creamed coconut, chopped
600 ml/1 pint double cream
225 g/8 oz icing sugar
2 bananas
1 tsp lemon juice
fresh fruit, to serve

method

1 Put the creamed coconut in a small bowl. Add just enough boiling water to cover and stir until dissolved. Set aside until cool.

2 Whip the cream with the sugar until thick but still floppy. Mash the bananas with the lemon juice and whisk gently into the cream, along with the cold coconut.

3 Transfer to a freezerproof container and freeze overnight. Serve in scoops with fresh fruit.

pistachio ice cream

ingredients

SERVES 4

300 ml/10 fl oz double cream
150 g/5½ oz thick natural yogurt
2 tbsp milk
3 tbsp honey
green food colouring
55 g/2 oz shelled unsalted pistachio nuts, finely chopped

pistachio praline

oil, for brushing
150 g/5½ oz granulated sugar
3 tbsp water
55 g/2 oz shelled, whole, unsalted pistachio nuts

method

1 Set the freezer to its lowest setting. Put the cream, yogurt, milk and honey in a bowl and mix together. Add a few drops of green food colouring to tint the mixture pale green and stir in well. Pour the mixture into a shallow freezer container and freeze, uncovered, for 1–2 hours or until beginning to set around the edges. Turn the mixture into a bowl and, with a fork, stir until smooth and then stir in the pistachio nuts. Return to the freezer container, cover and freeze for a further 2–3 hours or until firm. Alternatively, use an ice cream maker, following the manufacturer's instructions.

2 To make the pistachio praline, brush a baking sheet with oil. Put the sugar and water in a saucepan and heat gently, stirring, until the sugar has dissolved, then allow to bubble gently, without stirring, for 6–10 minutes or until light golden brown.

3 Remove the pan from the heat and stir in the pistachio nuts. Immediately pour the mixture onto the baking sheet and spread out evenly. Stand in a cool place for about 1 hour, until cold and hardened, then crush it in a plastic bag with a hammer.

4 About 30 minutes before serving, remove the ice cream from the freezer and stand at room temperature to soften slightly. To serve, scatter the praline over the ice cream.

cinnamon ice cream

ingredients

SERVES 4–6

300 ml/10 fl oz whipping cream

1 tsp ground cinnamon

600 ml/1 pint carton fresh custard

1 tbsp lemon juice

100 g/3½ oz icing sugar

method

1 Pour the cream into a heavy-based saucepan, add the ground cinnamon and stir together. Bring almost to the boil, then remove from the heat and infuse for 30 minutes.

2 Put the custard and lemon juice in a large bowl. Sift in the icing sugar, then stir together. Pour in the cinnamon cream and whisk together until mixed.

3 If using an ice cream maker, churn the mixture in the machine following the manufacturer's instructions. Alternatively, freeze the mixture in a freezerproof container, uncovered, for 1–2 hours, or until it starts to set around the edges.

4 Turn the mixture into a bowl and stir with a fork or beat in a food processor until smooth. Return to the freezer and freeze for a further 2–3 hours, or until firm or required. Cover the container with a lid for storing.

maple syrup & walnut ice cream

ingredients

SERVES 6

115 g/4 oz walnut pieces

150 ml/5 fl oz maple syrup

300 ml/10 fl oz double cream

200 ml/7 fl oz canned evaporated milk, well chilled

method

1 Process the walnut pieces in a food processor until finely chopped but be careful not to process them into a purée. Set aside.

2 Mix the syrup and cream together until well blended. Pour the chilled evaporated milk into a large bowl and whisk until thick and doubled in volume. The mixture should leave a trail when the whisk is lifted. Add the syrup mixture to the whisked milk and fold together.

3 If using an ice cream maker, churn the mixture in the machine following the manufacturer's instructions. Just before the ice cream freezes, add the chopped nuts. Alternatively, freeze the mixture in a freezerproof container, uncovered, for 1–2 hours or until it starts to set around the edges. Turn the mixture into a bowl and stir with a fork or beat in a food processor until smooth. Stir in the chopped nuts, then return to the freezer and freeze for a further 2–3 hours or until firm or required. Cover the container with a lid for storing.

dark chocolate ice cream

ingredients

SERVES 6

2 eggs

2 egg yolks

115 g/4 oz golden caster sugar

300 ml/10 fl oz single cream

225 g/8 oz plain chocolate, chopped

300 ml/10 fl oz double cream

4 tbsp brandy

method

1 Place the whole eggs, egg yolks and sugar in a heatproof bowl and beat together until well blended. Place the single cream and chocolate in a saucepan and heat gently until the chocolate has melted, then continue to heat, stirring constantly, until almost boiling. Pour onto the egg mixture, stirring vigorously, then set the bowl over a pan of gently simmering water, making sure that the base of the bowl does not touch the water.

2 Cook, stirring constantly, until the mixture lightly coats the back of the spoon. Strain into a separate bowl and cool. Place the double cream and brandy in a separate bowl and whip until slightly thickened, then fold into the cooled chocolate mixture.

3 Freeze in an ice cream maker, following the manufacturer's instructions. Alternatively, pour the mixture into a large freezerproof container, then cover and freeze for 2 hours or until just frozen. Spoon into a bowl and beat with a fork to break down the ice crystals. Return to the freezer for 2 hours or until firm. Transfer the ice cream to the refrigerator 30 minutes before serving. Scoop the ice cream into 4 serving dishes or coffee cups and serve.

chocolate & honey ice cream

ingredients

SERVES 6

500 ml/18 fl oz milk
200 g/7 oz plain chocolate, broken into pieces
4 eggs, separated
85 g/3 oz caster sugar
pinch of salt
2 tbsp honey
12 fresh strawberries, washed and hulled

method

1 Pour the milk into a pan, add 150 g/5½ oz of the chocolate and stir over medium heat for 3–5 minutes or until melted. Remove the pan from the heat and set aside.

2 Beat the egg yolks with all but 1 tablespoon of the sugar in a separate bowl until pale and thickened. Gradually beat in the milk mixture, a little at a time. Return the mixture to a clean pan and cook over low heat, whisking constantly, until smooth and thickened. Remove from the heat and cool. Cover with clingfilm and chill in the refrigerator for 30 minutes.

3 Whisk the egg whites with a pinch of salt until soft peaks form. Gradually whisk in the remaining sugar and whisk until stiff and glossy. Stir the honey into the chocolate mixture, then gently fold in the egg whites. Divide between 6 individual freezerproof moulds and freeze for at least 4 hours.

4 Meanwhile, melt the remaining chocolate until smooth in a heatproof bowl set over a saucepan of barely simmering water. Half coat the strawberries in the melted chocolate. Place on a sheet of baking parchment to set. Transfer the ice cream to the refrigerator for 10 minutes before serving. Serve decorated with the chocolate-coated strawberries.

marshmallow ice cream

ingredients

SERVES 4

85 g/3 oz plain chocolate, broken into pieces

175 g/6 oz white marshmallows

150 ml/5 fl oz milk

300 ml/10 fl oz double cream

method

1 Put the plain chocolate and marshmallows in a saucepan and pour in the milk. Warm over very low heat until the chocolate and marshmallows have melted. Remove from the heat and cool completely.

2 Whisk the cream until thick, then fold it into the cold chocolate mixture with a metal spoon. Pour into a 450-g/1-lb loaf tin and freeze for at least 2 hours or until firm (it will keep for 1 month in the freezer). Serve the ice cream with fresh fruit.

mango sorbet

ingredients

SERVES 4–6

2 large ripe mangoes
juice of 1 lemon
pinch of salt
100 g/3½ oz sugar
3 tbsp water

method

1 Thinly peel the mangoes, holding them over a bowl to catch the juices. Cut the flesh away from the central stone and put in a food processor or blender. Add the mango juice, lemon juice and salt and process to form a smooth purée. Push the mango purée through a nylon sieve into the bowl.

2 Put the sugar and water in a heavy-based saucepan and heat gently, stirring, until the sugar has dissolved. Bring to the boil, without stirring, then remove the pan from the heat and cool slightly.

3 Pour the syrup into the mango purée and mix well together. Cool the mango syrup, then chill in the refrigerator for 2 hours, until cold.

4 If using an ice cream maker, churn the mixture in the machine following the manufacturer's instructions. Alternatively, freeze the mixture in a freezerproof container, uncovered, for 3–4 hours or until mushy. Turn the mixture into a bowl and stir with a fork or beat in a food processor to break down the ice crystals. Return to the freezer and freeze for a further 3–4 hours, or until firm or required. Cover the container with a lid for storing.

pineapple & lime sorbet

ingredients

SERVES 4

225 g/8 oz caster sugar
600 ml/1 pint water
grated rind and juice of 2 limes
1 small pineapple, peeled, quartered and chopped
sweet biscuits, to serve

method

1 Put the sugar and water into a saucepan and heat gently, stirring until the sugar has dissolved. Bring to the boil and simmer for 10 minutes.

2 Stir in the grated rind and half the lime juice. Remove from the heat and cool.

3 Put the pineapple in a blender or food processor and process until smooth. Add to the cold syrup with the remaining lime juice. Pour into a freezerproof container and freeze until crystals have formed around the edge.

4 Turn out the sorbet into a bowl. Beat well with a fork to break up the crystals. Return to the freezer and chill overnight. Serve in scoops with sweet biscuits.

gooseberry & elderflower sorbet

ingredients

SERVES 6

100 g/3½ oz sugar
600 ml/1 pint water
500 g/1 lb 2 oz fresh gooseberries
125 ml/4 fl oz elderflower cordial
1 tbsp lemon juice
few drops of green food colouring (optional)
125 ml/4 fl oz double cream

method

1 Put the sugar and water in a heavy-based saucepan and heat gently, stirring, until the sugar has dissolved. Bring to the boil, then add the gooseberries, without trimming them, and simmer, stirring occasionally, for 10 minutes or until very tender. Cool for 5 minutes.

2 Put the gooseberries in a food processor or blender and process to form a smooth purée. Push the purée through a nylon sieve into a bowl to remove the seeds. Cool for at least 1 hour.

3 Add the elderflower cordial and lemon juice to the cold gooseberry purée and stir together until well mixed. If wished, add the food colouring to tint the mixture pale green. Stir the cream into the mixture.

4 If using an ice cream maker, churn the mixture in the machine following the manufacturer's instructions. Alternatively, freeze the mixture in a freezerproof container, uncovered, for 3–4 hours or until mushy. Turn the mixture into a bowl and stir with a fork or beat in a food processor to break down the ice crystals. Return to the freezer and freeze for a further 3–4 hours or until firm. Cover the container with a lid for storing.

red berry sorbet

ingredients

SERVES 6

175 g/6 oz redcurrants, plus extra to decorate
175 g/6 oz raspberries, plus extra to decorate
175 m/6 fl oz water
100 g/3½ oz sugar
150 ml/5 fl oz cranberry juice
2 egg whites

method

1 Strip the redcurrants from their stalks using the prongs of a fork and put them in a large heavy-based saucepan together with the raspberries. Add 2 tablespoons of the water and cook over medium heat for 10 minutes or until soft. Push the fruit through a nylon sieve into a bowl to form a purée.

2 Put the sugar and the remaining water into the rinsed-out pan and heat gently, stirring, until the sugar has dissolved. Bring to the boil, then boil, without stirring, for 10 minutes to form a syrup. Do not let it brown. Remove from the heat and cool for at least 1 hour. When cold, stir the fruit purée and cranberry juice into the syrup.

3 If using an ice cream maker, churn the mixture in the machine following the manufacturer's instructions. When the mixture starts to freeze, whisk the egg whites until they just hold their shape but are not dry, then add to the mixture and continue churning. Serve sprinkled with extra fruits.

berry yogurt ice

ingredients

SERVES 4

125 g/4 1/2 oz raspberries
125 g/4 1/2 oz blackberries
125 g/4 1/2 oz strawberries
1 large egg
175 ml/6 fl oz thick natural yogurt
125 ml/4 fl oz red wine
2 1/4 tsp powdered gelatine
fresh berries, to decorate

method

1 Place the raspberries, blackberries and strawberries in a blender or food processor and process until a smooth purée forms. Rub the purée through a sieve into a bowl to remove the seeds.

2 Break the egg and separate the yolk and white into separate bowls. Stir the egg yolk and yogurt into the berry purée and set the egg white aside.

3 Pour the wine into a heatproof bowl set over a saucepan of water. Sprinkle the gelatine on the surface of the wine and stand for 5 minutes to soften. Heat the pan of water and simmer until the gelatine has dissolved. Pour the mixture into the berry purée in a steady stream, whisking constantly. Transfer the mixture to a freezerproof container and freeze for 2 hours or until slushy.

4 Whisk the egg white in a spotlessly clean, greasefree bowl until very stiff. Remove the berry mixture from the freezer and fold in the egg white. Return to the freezer and freeze for 2 hours or until firm.

5 To serve, scoop the berry yogurt ice into glass dishes and decorate with fresh berries of your choice.

lemon water ice

ingredients

SERVES 6

200 g/7 oz sugar

425 ml/15 fl oz water

6–9 large lemons

lemon slices, to decorate

method

1 Put the sugar and water in a heavy-based saucepan and heat gently, stirring, until the sugar has dissolved. Bring to the boil, then boil, without stirring, for 10 minutes to form a syrup. Do not let it brown.

2 Meanwhile, using a potato peeler, thinly pare the rind from 4 of the lemons. Remove the syrup from the heat and add the pared lemon rind. Cool for at least 1 hour.

3 Squeeze the juice from the lemons and strain into a measuring cup – you need 425 ml/15 fl oz in total. When the syrup is cold, strain it into a bowl, add the lemon juice and stir together until well mixed.

4 If using an ice cream maker, churn the mixture in the machine following the manufacturer's instructions. Alternatively, freeze the mixture in a freezerproof container, uncovered, for 3–4 hours or until mushy. Turn the mixture into a bowl and stir with a fork or beat in a food processor to break down the ice crystals. Return to the freezer and freeze for a further 3–4 hours or until firm. Cover the container with a lid for storing. Serve decorated with lemon slices.

coffee granita

ingredients

SERVES 6

2 tbsp sugar

600 ml/1 pint water

55 g/2 oz fresh Italian coffee, finely ground

125 ml/4 fl oz whipping cream, whipped, to serve

method

1 Put the sugar and water in a heavy-based saucepan and heat gently, stirring, until the sugar has dissolved. Bring to the boil, then remove from the heat and stir in the coffee. Infuse and cool for 1 hour.

2 Strain the coffee through a paper filter or a sieve lined with cheesecloth. Pour the coffee into 2 shallow freezerproof containers and freeze, uncovered, for 30 minutes.

3 Turn both mixtures into a bowl and stir with a fork or beat in a food processor to break down the ice crystals. Return to the freezer and freeze, repeating the breaking down of the ice crystals about every 30 minutes until the granita is granular. This process will take 3–4 hours in total. Cover the container with a lid for storing.

4 Serve the granita in glasses, straight from the freezer, broken into tiny ice crystals. Top each glass with a little whipped cream.

chocolate sorbet

ingredients

SERVES 6

55 g/2 oz cocoa powder
150 g/5½ oz golden caster sugar
2 tsp instant coffee powder
2 cups water
crisp biscuits, to serve

method

1 Sift the cocoa powder into a small, heavy-based saucepan and add the caster sugar, coffee powder and a little of the water. Using a wooden spoon, mix together to form a thin paste, then gradually stir in the remaining water. Bring the mixture to the boil over low heat and simmer gently for 8 minutes, stirring frequently.

2 Remove the pan from the heat and cool. Transfer the mixture to a bowl, cover with clingfilm and place in the refrigerator until well chilled. Freeze in an ice cream maker, following the manufacturer's instructions. Alternatively, pour the mixture into a large freezerproof container, then cover and freeze for 2 hours. Remove the sorbet from the freezer and beat to break down the ice crystals. Freeze for a further 6 hours, beating the sorbet every 2 hours.

3 Transfer the sorbet to the refrigerator 30 minutes before serving. Scoop into 6 small bowls and serve with crisp biscuits.